MAPPING YOUR ADVENTURE

DISCOVERING INTEGRITY IN A LIFE REVIEW

D. MARK COOPER

MAPPING YOUR ADVENTURE:
DISCOVERING INTEGRITY IN A LIFE REVIEW
Written by D. Mark Cooper
Copyright © 2016 D. Mark Cooper

Published by
Bluebullseye Press
bluebullseyepress.com
A division of Bluebullseye LLC

ISBN: 978-0-9975670-2-1

All rights reserved. This book, or parts thereof, may
not be reproduced in any form without permission.

No part of this publication may be reproduced or
transmitted in any form or by any means, mechanical or
electronic, including photocopying or recording, or by any
information storage and retrieval system, or transmitted
by email without permission in writing from the author.

Neither the author nor the publisher assumes any
responsibility for errors, omissions, or contrary
interpretations of the subject matter herein. Any
perceived slight of any individual or organization is purely
unintentional.

Brand and product names are trademarks or registered
trademarks of their respective owners.

Edited by Ginger Moran

Cover design by John H. Matthews, bluebullseyepress.com

Dedicated to:

Jennifer L. Porter
Katherine A. Ford
Laura A. Cooper

Writing this memoir has been an exercise in learning how to become a writer. I have more to learn. But I have had help and much support along the way.

My children, their husbands and their children are my most important support and being involved in their lives is a daily joy. My friend Christine Stoughton has been in my life only a short time in the sum total, but I value her friendship and I marvel at her insight and her art.

The Rector at Sr. James's Episcopal Church, Richmond, Virginia, Randy Hollerith, has been a major support. His welcome to St. James and his invitation to serve on staff in various roles was a true honor. The staff and members of that community have been a major source of support and I hold them in highest esteem. The Men's Bible Class was there for me in some of the darkest days. It is a privilege to study with that group.

Ron Qualley, recently retired Senior Pastor at Lord of Life Lutheran Church in Fairfax, Virginia was another significant support in the years of my professional work. We shared a deep love for the people of that parish and he supported my work in Adult Education.

Dean Cecil Drain and Senior Associate Dean Alexander Tarteglia of the School of Allied Health Care Professions of Virginia Commonwealth University invited me to return to Richmond and to Clinical Pastoral Education. It was an honor to serve on the faculty under their direction.

Finally, Ginger Moran, Ph. D. has recently come into my life as a coach, editor and friend. She has been a true guide through the process of finishing this memoir. She pulled together the team that made this book possible and I very much appreciate her encouragement, expertise and oversight.

There are always more people to thank and I have been richly blessed.

TABLE OF CONTENTS

INTRODUCTION 1

PART 1
THE FIRST FOUR STAGES - FORMATION OF THE MIND   5
- STAGE ONE: BASIC TRUST VS. BASIC MISTRUST   6
- QUESTIONS FOR STAGE ONE   15
- STAGE TWO: AUTONOMY VS. SHAME AND DOUBT   16
- QUESTIONS FOR STAGE TWO   20
- STAGE THREE: INITIATIVE VS. GUILT   21
- QUESTIONS FOR STAGE THREE   26
- STAGE FOUR: INDUSTRY VS. INFERIORITY   27
- QUESTIONS FOR STAGE FOUR   38

PART 2
STAGES FIVE AND SIX -
WHERE SPIRIT CONTINUES TO DEVELOP   39
- STAGE FIVE: IDENTITY VS. ROLE CONFUSION   40
- QUESTIONS FOR STAGE FIVE   59
- STAGE SIX: INTIMACY VS. ISOLATION   60
- QUESTIONS FOR STAGE SIX   92

PART 3
STAGES SEVEN AND EIGHT -
THE TIME OF THE BODY   93
- STAGE SEVEN: GENERATIVITY VS. STAGNATION   94
- QUESTIONS FOR STAGE SEVEN   153
- STAGE EIGHT: EGO INTEGRITY VS. DESPAIR   154

ABOUT THE AUTHOR   **175**

MAPPING YOUR ADVENTURE

DISCOVERING INTEGRITY IN A LIFE REVIEW

INTRODUCTION

Getting old is a bitch, but it beats the alternative.

I hate the word "retirement." What does it mean? "Re" suggests that you are going to do something again, or you are referring to something. So are you going to do another tire, or do you want to do something with a tire—like putting on new Michelins or taking on the Goodyear Blimp?

At a gut level "retirement" suggests lying down, giving up, coming to the end of work and walking away. I like work. I enjoy getting things done. I've retired three times and each time the next day I was at work at another job.

Don't get me wrong. I enjoy the going away parties and the recognition of work well done. But I'm not giving up. I have no interest in sitting on some porch somewhere drinking mint juleps (though I've never tried one—maybe there's hope yet). I find work to be a place where I can see things happen. At work I share with others the hopes and dreams for making change, creating something.

Earlier in my career there was always a struggle over choosing between my home life and my work life. I enjoyed both. I liked being with my wife and watching our kids grow up. It was hard to go back to the office after the paternity leave ran out. Vacations were fun, and on weekends I looked forward to being at swim meets, cutting the grass, going to movies, or having dinner with friends. But on Monday I enjoyed going to the office. I had a whole different family there. We worked and dreamed and saw things happen and things that failed. I liked the money I was paid. I tried to do my best in every job to deserve what I received.

But now here I am 72 years old, not working a "regular" job, in good health, a widower. I have Social Security and a pension, no mortgage, little debt. My mind is clear when I can remember where the keys are and what your name is. So this time when I retired I decided to claim my new identity as a writer.

I have been a writer all of my life. Even as a child I can remember a time on a sun porch when I was scribbling lines on blank paper, handing it to my Grandma who read back what I had written. When I turned 50 and after 25 years as an ordained clergy I rode a bike across the USA with two other guys and I wrote a book called *Get a Life: A Second Chance After Fifty*. I had started my own consulting company and was working with men and women who were being "right- sized" out of their lifelong careers. I developed a series of lectures on how to get back in the game and I talked those lectures into my computer. My co-author and I self-published the book. I planned to use the book in my work with clients who were in job transitions. It was a good "leave behind" in my work with individuals and group and a good summary of thing I had learned in my contact with people in job change. But then I was called to another job.

This time when I retired for the third or fourth time I decided to do it differently. In the past each time something had developed that provided the next place to go. The good thing about those opportunities was the structure they provided. I had an office and work was expected from me. I also had a group of peers that I worked with. For one as extroverted as I am, having people around is important. But this time I decided to go on my own. I returned to my writing dream.

In writing the book about career development one of the chapters that I included was a review of the work of Erik Erikson. In 1950 he published a book called *Childhood and Society*. A chapter was called "Eight Stages of Man." I presented those stages in my first book as a way for the reader to begin a self-analysis.

Erikson believed that personality developed in stages. Just as the fetus in utero had developed in stages, he believed that our personality after we are born followed a sequence of stages. Each stage had a crisis point. The personality could resolve the crisis on a healthy side or on a weaker side. Regardless of the choice, from that point on the personality would be affected by that resolution.

In my work over the years with people in pastoral care I have found it useful to invite them to do a life review. How has life been to this point, what has been accomplished, what remains to be done? I now want to come back to those stages and in effect do what I asked other people to do. I am going to use my own life and experiences as illustrations of my process through those stages as an example of how one might do this sort of life experience inventory. I ask you now to come along with me on this journey.

Erikson's last stage is called "Integrity Vs. Despair." The various decisions we make as we go through life build toward this last one. It is important to review the stages leading up to this one so that we can launch into it with a sense of lively, dynamic integrity rather than sinking into a tired despair.

Forty-five years and one week after my ordination as a Lutheran Pastor I preached my last sermon as an Interim Associate Rector in an Episcopal Church. How I got from a beginning in Columbia, South Carolina to that church in Richmond, Virginia, is the content of this book. I have not followed the expected course, I have been very fortunate, and I've learned a lot a long the way. On the surface my life has appeared to be successful and in general I feel good about where I've been and what I've been able to do. But it has not been a straight line. In many ways as I look back I have failed as often as I succeeded. I have had some significant teachers and as a result of those relationships developed a sense of permission to learn on my own, to follow my own intuition. I also had some significant opportunities to be in a leadership role and gave them my best effort. As I come into this next stage of life I want to reflect on that past, to try and understand what happened and to look for threads that might be helpful for others to consider.

PART 1

THE FIRST FOUR STAGES - FORMATION OF THE MIND

In the first four stages of life we start at birth with innocent awareness and grow through these first stages into growing awareness. We are learning more each day about the plasticity of the human brain. As our bodies grow and develop so does our capacity to think and to understand our feelings. We don't achieve real maturity until we are at least 30 years old, well into our lives by that time. The experiences we have in these first years lay down tracks that will become part of who we are well into our final days. As you read about these stages, think about your early experiences, talk to your siblings and your peers. What do they remember about your childhood and adolescent experiences? Think about the cross roads that occurred in your life that set you on the course for becoming the person you are today.

STAGE ONE: BASIC TRUST VS. BASIC MISTRUST

> *"Trust born of care is, in fact, the touchstone of actuality of a given religion."*
> Erik H. Erikson, *Childhood and Society*

There is nothing like the experience of holding a new born child, looking into their eyes, knowing that as they look back you are being seen for the first time and are seeing for the first time. Much goes into that first moment. Who is this child? What will he or she become? What lies ahead and what has come with them from the past into this new being? The first quarter of life is one of significant growth physically, emotionally, and mentally. Some of the experiences can be programed and provided, but what this child will do with what happens from this moment on is yet to be revealed. The foundation is being laid with this first meeting and years later will reveal some of the answers that this first meeting engenders.

Erikson's suggests that in the first months to a year of childhood the new infant is completely dependent on their environment for life. If the child is cared for and the environment is trustworthy, the emerging ego of the child will likely become trusting as well.

I will now look at how this applies in my life and invite you to do the same.

A little background on my environment

Lutherans came to this country in the 1700's when the German and French settled one of their many wars by declaring an open space between the borders of the two countries. The Germans who lived in that buffer zone were forced to abandon their homes and property to move to England. That turned out to be a temporary move and The Queen sent these immigrants to the new world. As a result of those moves there are Lutheran communities extending from New York through Point of Rocks, Virginia, down into North and South Carolina. The British citizens who lived on the coast and in the middle of those territories did not want the Germans in their communities and forced them to move up into the mountains and Valley that was in the western part of those states.

While doing some work on my family tree I discovered pre-Revolutionary gravesites at the Lutheran Church at Point of Rocks, Virginia that had the name Cooper on the stones. I could not make a definite connection to my family, but there were Coopers in Rowan County, North Carolina that did connect.

The Coopers made the barrels, the hog heads for corn later converted to drink and other storage needs. My great grandfather Cooper owned the roller mill in China Grove, North Carolina, and those Coopers had ten children, many of whom had distinguished careers in the years that followed. My granddad and grandmother were from that community and had been part of that Lutheran tradition. In that community they would have been part of the elite. Granddad had a master's degree in history and grandmother had been to a junior college for a time. They married and moved to High Point, North Carolina and had their two children. Dad went to college in that town and for a time was an editor of the college newspaper and a tennis player. One of the pictures in the family album is of my dad holding me as his dad and grandfather look on, four generations of Lutheran men on a Sunday afternoon no doubt after church and a family lunch.

My dad was ordained to Lutheran ministry in 1942. His first call was as an assistant pastor at St. Mark's Lutheran Church in Charlotte, North Carolina. He had not been able to join the fight in Europe during World War II because he had been born with missing fingers and a problem with his hip that necessitated surgery in his childhood and as a result one leg was shorter than the other and he needed for a built up shoe. He used his skills as the editor of his college newspaper for the rest of his life as the editor of various church newspapers popular during his ministry. He was the president of the North Carolina Luther League during his college years and was an up and coming new clergy. He had come from an established family of Lutherans who lived in central North Carolina.

The day of the four-generation picture may have been the day of my baptism; the white gown that I was dressed in would be the type of required dress for that service. In the Lutheran tradition Baptism is considered a sacrament and is a time when the congregation promises with the parents of the child brought to the font that they would raise this child in the Christian tradition. The child becomes a part of the church "family."

Later in my work in ministry I would have occasion to participate in baptisms including the ones for my grandchildren. For me there was serious meaning in that congregational commitment. The child was not alone and not only a member of their birth parents' immediate family, but also of a larger group of people who would claim that child as one of their own. When I hold one of those children and with one hand splash water from the basin onto their heads I am connecting them to a long tradition, to a community that shares common beliefs and commitments. How that commitment gets lived out depends on the family. The church provides Sunday Schools and teachers from the congregation and inclusion in the activities of the church. Later it will provide confirmation, a class that tries to communicate the basic beliefs of the church and asks the child now to take responsibility for their own faith. I have felt a connection to the community of the church all of my life; it is hard for me to imagine who I am a part from that life long connection.

My mother was the oldest daughter of Ethyl and William Goodwin who were members of St. Mark's Lutheran Church. They had moved to Charlotte during the years of the Depression when William's print shop failed and they lost their home and furniture along with the business. They had also suffered the loss of two children to early childhood disease. There was a gap between my mother and her brother of some years. Mother was a tall beauty who had finished college in a small woman's school in South Carolina, Coker College. She graduated in science and had written some poetry while in college. After college she traveled to Richmond, Virginia to study in the William and Mary Master's in Social Work program. She left after a year without finishing the degree.

My mother's brother did some research on their family history and found an interesting story that has some credibility to it. Supposedly Sir Walter Raleigh had been in negotiation with a tribe on Indians on the coast of North Carolina, an Algonquian tribe. He is said to have traded two of his cabin boys with the chief for two of the tribe's boys. Twenty years later there is a record of a Goodwin man married to an Algonquian woman in that same area. That story was never confirmed but, given that the women of the tribe were tall and strong, at least my uncle believed that my mother must have been a descendent of that tribe.

Grandma's family was a deep-South family that at one time had had slaves that had given them up after the Civil War. Her family's patriarch had entered Philadelphia in 1730, a Peterson; he was a Methodist minister who migrated to the Carolinas.

My parents first date was a tennis match. My dad's shorter leg did not deter his ability to put himself fully into tennis, an interest that he would pursue all of his life. He must have wanted the approval of this woman—he did not slam the ball on his serve in ways that I remember his slams later on. They married in 1942. It didn't take me long to get here. I was born in 1943.

The infant at this stage is totally dependent on the caregivers that are around; without them you cannot survive. The concept "good enough parenting" suggests that at this stage if, when a child is hungry they are fed, when they need a diaper changed it is changed and when they need to be held someone holds them, then they can trust their environment. If there is that level of interaction, a responsive environment to the needs of the child, then trust can evolve. If you are not held when you are hungry, put to bed when you are sleepy, changed when you need to be held, trust may not develop.

While it was never discussed I think that my mother found being a mother to be difficult. I suspect that my dad's sister and his mother stepped in along with mother's mother to take care of me in the early months. But in general I think that I ended up on the trusting side.

Erikson also suggests that this first stage is the beginning of faith. If you cannot trust those who are first responsible for you, how can you come to trust in a God you can't see or in a community that promises to be there for you and may not in fact be there at times of need? I can tell by my belief that environment must have proven to be trustworthy. As I mentioned, there was extended family close by if my mother was not as available. Though there is some question about my connection to the Algonquian Indian tribe I like the feeling of being connected to those natives along with the clear connection to the Germans who were displaced from their homes and came to this country to carve out their continued existence. At one point it was important to me as an adult to research those early roots and to find links to my own way of being. Our family survived the ups and downs of life in this new country and those of a long-term connection to the church. Raising my own three daughters in the community of the church gave me a sense that those people did reach out to infants: children were passed around and loved, held and fed. It happened for my children and I can only assume that my young parents were invited to turn their children over to the care of the congregation. There was every reason to trust in the world we were born into, little reason to be afraid.

Two years later when my brother was born we had moved again to another small town and to a single church. We lived next door to the church and had to get up and out early on Sunday morning because the church was growing and needed to have places to meet for Sunday school. Mother did not like having to open her home every Sunday as members of the church filed in for their classes. Dad led the church through the building of an educational building.

My first memory as a child was playing around the excavation for that building. The gray Ford tractor with its red engine was a particular interest. It had a unique smell of oil, grease and exhaust that I can recall when I see one of those old tractors that are now collector's items. I remember joining my parents behind a wall as we watched the dynamite blow up the rock so that a basement could be dug. I later fell into one of the holes that had been dug and one of the worker's was heard to remark, "Leave him in there for a while. We need a break."

These were good years for the family and the community. The war was winding down, the economy had picked up. Grandma declared that she would for the rest of her life vote Democratic because of President Roosevelt and what he had done to restore the economy. Interestingly, my parents were Republican for most of those early years because that party was the one of Lincoln. It was more liberal toward the black community. Everyone could remember someone who would not be returning from the wars in Europe and Asia. Years later mother would talk of men she had dated who were killed during that time. There was wistfulness around those reveries. I don't know if mother regretted those losses or the opportunities they would have offered. Those who did return had the G.I. Bill and began to build their new homes and lives around a growing economy.

Farming was central and surrounded the town that provided stores and business that supported the work of the area. The pastor in that community was an automatic leader and was respected as such. Service clubs like the Lions and Rotary were gatherings for men that were both social and community service in orientation. While the salary for a clergy may not have been significant, the provision of a parsonage, and discounts for clothes, a car, and food were expectations that allowed the pastor's family to live a solid middle class life. Every quarter our home was "pounded" when the members of the church would come and fill our pantry with all sorts of products from their farms.

My dad was a bright man who was becoming a leader in the North Carolina church and he enjoyed good relationships with other clergy in the area. He wrote out his sermons each week and was from the beginning one who read theology and continued his education. Mother seems to have been lost in the process; she was not a Southern cook and did not seem to enjoy the role of hostess. She did not pursue work outside our home in those early years.

It has occurred only recently to me that I grew up in a somewhat ethnic community. We were part of a congregation of fellow Lutherans who were descendants of those early German migrants. While we all spoke English and services were in English, there were churches around that held on to their German language and services. My friends were from the church. My neighbors were part of that community. When I would go to college it would be to a Lutheran school. Lutherans married Lutherans, did business with Lutherans, took care of their own and didn't open their doors to others except as visiting missionaries that had stories to tell and requests to make, but they weren't invited into membership.

Are you basically trusting or untrusting?
If your early childhood was disrupted or difficult you might have trouble trusting others in your adult life. If you do you already know that this is a difficult concern. Not being able to trust can keep you from moving forward, taking risks, making commitments. But I don't believe that your environment or early childhood experiences are cast in stone. I've heard other therapists say that if you don't like the family you had, create another family that is more like the one you need. Over the years I have met people who are naturally able to be nurturing. My wife's mother was one of those people for me. She was not a big talker, but she expressed her care in her cooking and in her care for our children. The community of a church can be a place of welcome and of shared care. Grandparents whose children live in other communities may find enjoyment in grandparenting the children of the church. A mentor at work could give you the opportunity to trust and in having that experience find it easier to generalize that feeling in a larger world. If you find yourself unsure about another person or relationship, think about who that person is and whether or not they are truly trustworthy. If they are, take a risk. You may be hurt, but you will learn from the experience. And if it works out it will help you expand your world of trust to a wider world.

QUESTIONS FOR STAGE ONE

As you think back or ask about the time of your birth here are some questions to consider:

1. What was the environment you grew up in?
2. How did it affect your developing mind?
3. What are some of the familial traits that have been handed down?
4. Did you grow up in a religious environment? How has that affected your development?
5. Have you taken a look at your family's genealogy? Was there any impact you can discern on your development?

STAGE TWO: AUTONOMY VS. SHAME AND DOUBT

> "The sense of autonomy fostered in the child and modified as life progresses serves (and is served by) the preservation in economic and political life of a sense of justice."
> Erik H. Erikson, *Childhood and Society*

The infant is now starting to move around—first crawling, pulling up, then walking. They become more independent. One minute they are engaged in one thing, the next minute they have disappeared. The child steps out away from the parent but looks back to be sure that the adult is not far away.

Erikson's second stage is one of "Autonomy vs. Shame/Doubt." This stage starts around age two and lasts for a couple of years.

For me this starts with the birth of my brother Paul. Having now had three children of my own and five grand children, I see this stage more clearly. The two year old is moving from being held to being mobile, from crawling to walking and in most cases to running. There seem to be no restraints in the child's mind, crawling over things, falling down, pushing, and pulling, on the move.

I was born in a time when children were supposed to be seen and not heard. That model didn't fit me well. One story that survived early childhood was of my escape from home when I was two. Somehow during the night I left home and went next door to a neighbor's to get candy. I can imagine my parent's chagrin when they were awakened and I was returned. No doubt the messages were not subtle about the shame I was bringing to the family. My dad's mother added to those feelings. She already felt that her daughter-in-law was beneath her son's station in life and now this first son was too active, too loud and later she would consider me overweight. On the other side I was the first grandchild and as such had a special place in the family.

After a lot of reflection and therapy I know that I resolved this stage on the more negative side. I can find shame in a moment especially in my early adulthood around those in authority. I tend to approach new environments with some caution, looking for the rules, the expectations before I express myself more openly. As an adult I began to recognize when I was feeling shame and in the recognition could began to reclaim my autonomy.

Erikson believed that a negative resolution would always be there. In therapy you can work back to that initial resolution and understand its impact, but it will continue to be part of who you are and how you deal with stress. That has certainly been true for me. Each time I have moved into a new stage of potential accomplishment, I have had shame threaten my advancement. Even now when I think of myself as a writer, I can claim that skill as a vocation. But part of me has a feeling that I am not really a writer and that my subterfuge will be discovered. At that point I would be shamed, so claiming the title of writer is something I hold onto with my fingernails.

This is a stage that we all understand and see manifested around us when young children are involved. Today there is a great deal of openness in allowing for self-expression and the development of a strong sense of individuality, unlike when I was growing up. It was clear in my family that one was not supposed to "get a big head" and the consequences for being too loud or assertive were sometimes harsh. Shame was a common theme. I think that I did develop a healthy sense of myself, but that I learned to suppress or hide in order to fit into my larger family's expectation. I was a "good" son and those parts of me that weren't so "good" were to be suppressed.

In resolving this crisis more on the negative side, according to Erikson's stages, when I am under stress, in a new environment or where a strong sense of autonomy is called for, I may initially experience feelings of shame. When I moved into leadership roles in youth group and in high school I did so by first observing the environment and taking on the jobs that no one else wanted. I discovered ways to express my autonomy by taking action, but in a covert way that would lead to acceptance later in a leadership role. I had watched my dad as a leader, and over time I had opportunities to step up as a patrol leader or leader of the local church youth group. Those experiences prepared me to take on larger responsibilities as I matured and even today the model of moving into a new environment and picking up the roles from the bottom of the organization is still a mode of operation for me.

It seems to me that the idea of sin gets connected with this stage. The feelings of the child are unfiltered. We have all witnessed the scene in the grocery store when a young child is denied whatever candy or toy they had to have. When their request is denied the response is a meltdown on the floor, feet kicking, screaming, crying. Today's sophisticated parent just lets the kid kick it out, knowing that they will soon turn their attention elsewhere, but they are learning limits. In my childhood a child would have been punished for showing those feelings.

"I'm going to take off my belt, or get a switch from the tree nearby," were statements commonly heard, and the physical expression would be meted out. Violence met with violence. Sin would be treated in the same way: easily identified. And the expectation of judgment was that sin was to be suppressed. I remember my dad's belt in my early childhood. Later he would just have to look my way with "his look" and I would quickly realize the error of my ways.

Where are you on the continuum between autonomy and shame or doubt?

What kind of two year old were you? There must be stories around about this time in your life. How do you see them knowing that this is the time when the basic core of who this new person will become is set?

Many of us struggle with issues left over from this stage. Adults who grew up in a shaming culture seem to take some pleasure as adults in bringing those negative feelings to others, especially small children. There are some people who are bullies and intimidate others. The feelings of helplessness are often left over from those childhood experiences. Stopping ourselves when we feel that helpless response and asking if in fact we are without resources may help us respond out of a stronger part of ourselves. We all feel a composite of child, parent, and adult feelings. Drawing on our adult feelings can help us confront the intimidator and if need be interrupt our own internal judge, the negative parental feelings that stop us in our tracks.

QUESTIONS FOR STAGE TWO

1. What are the childhood stories that are told about you?
2. Did you have some freedom to explore or were you watched closely?
3. How was discipline managed in your house, did your parents share the discipline or was one parent in charge?
4. Was anyone paying attention?

STAGE THREE: INITIATIVE VS. GUILT

> *"Everyone needs a sense of initiative for whatever he/she learns and does, from fruit-gathering to a system of enterprise."*
> Erik H. Erikson, *Childhood and Society*

As the child grows they grow in awareness of the internal thoughts/feelings that are conscious but not expressed. It is an easier time for the family. The child begins to learn how to get what they want and along with their success may come some feeling of unexpressed anger, sexual feelings, and dishonesty.

The third stage is one Erikson calls "Initiative Vs. Guilt." As the child grows in age and skill they begin to move away from the unrestrained impulse to a more aware stage. The child can see what they want and how to more toward it. Building on the trust and autonomy of the first two stages they are able to begin to engage the world more directly and to learn how to work within the system of their family and soon in the school systems. Not only can they know that they want something, they can also become aware of its inappropriateness. The ego function is developing that allows a choice in behavior over raw emotional expression. The screaming two year old who cannot be calmed when they aren't getting what they want now becomes the three or four year old who is able to figure out how to negotiate for what they want either directly or passively.

This was an easier stage for me; one of the advantages of not having a lot of parental attention was the opportunity to develop my own imagination. I don't have memories from this time in my life, but in retrospect I think that I was more affected by shame in the previous stage than in this next stage by guilt. One of my favorite pastimes as a child was to take my collection of Match Box cars out into the yard where I would develop communities where I could work out my imagination's expression.

Life was my biggest teacher—watching the adults in my environment, learning what was expected of me, what was good and not so good. As an adult I have been more a "do it and if need be apologize later" type of person. Once I figure out what the game is, I have been able to move ahead into play and haven't been aware of carrying lot of guilt around.

From those early roots our family grew and I moved through the early stages of personality development. Dad was restless. We moved again after the building program was completed. This time he became a member of a Lutheran college staff as a fund-raiser. He traveled the state preaching in various churches to find support for the college. I remember fragments of a sermon I heard preached in several churches that included a telephone conversation to God. I don't remember if God suggested that people support higher education, but I suspect that it was in there somewhere.

We lived in a small house on the outskirts of Hickory, North Carolina. The roads around the house were not paved and the dust from those roads was thick. These were the years of the polio epidemic and I remember a feeling of anxiety about that childhood plague. Dad was traveling and Mother's mother was a frequent visitor. Mother was broadsided in a car wreck that rolled the new Plymouth that Dad had acquired. She was not injured and soon after my third brother, Steve, joined my brother and me, six years after my birth.

Dad enjoyed his work and was considering a role as college chaplain, but Mother did not like the community, the house, or anything. Instead of a role at the college Dad took a call to become a mission developer in a small community in the mountains of the Pisgah National Forest near Brevard, North Carolina. The Lutheran Church of North Carolina had put together funds to support mission development. Men like my dad would go into new areas where Lutheran churches did not exist and attempt to develop a worshiping community. I remember the sense that what Dad was promoting in that little mountain town was an anomaly. Our worship service was more like that of the Catholic Church, but clearly Dad was not a celibate priest.

The church grew but mostly from families who had moved into the area bringing their Lutheran heritage with them. You didn't become a Lutheran unless you were born to it or married into it. Some of those who married in from the Baptist tradition became the most enthusiastic of the congregation. I remember a warm feeling of connection. There was a nationally recognized summer music camp in the community that brought in musical excellence every summer and our church drew on those talents for Sunday music. Mother was the organist in the early years.

The five years we spent in Brevard were good years. We moved into an old parsonage next door to the church that our congregation bought from the Presbyterian Church. The house was large and comfortable. My mother's parents visited often. My grandfather was a gregarious ad salesman for the Charlotte Observer and they brought a lot of energy to our home. My grandma would take me fishing, baiting the line and helping me take the little fish I hooked off the line. I don't remember cleaning them so we must have thrown them back. She also believed in hard work and she taught me how to clean up the messes that came from life. She and I cleaned out the basement of that old house and she would over time teach me how to clean a bathroom. She wasn't very tall, but her sprit was big and I felt that she responded to me as a real person.

Did you experience more initiative or more guilt?

Age four to five or six is a time of growing self-awareness. The child becomes aware of feeling or thoughts that are not necessarily expressed but have concreteness to them. You could be angry with a parent and could wish them harm but not express that feeling or act on it. It is the awareness that is available to the child. With that new awareness the children can also begin to assert themselves, to have a thought and act on it with positive results. In a sense it becomes a consolidation of the first three stages. Building on trust and autonomy, the child becomes more clearly who they are in relation to their world. Most children make it through those years with little trauma and their core personality is established.

Over the years I have worked with people whose presenting problems seem overwhelming, but in time we discover an underlying solidness from this early time and that core personality can be sustaining as the person works through the more recent experiences.

By this time in life the child is no longer a baby. They are now a little person who can think and reason. They are starting to put away the childish things of the past and copy even more the adult life that surrounds them.

Being weighed down by guilt is a difficult experience. Our religious tradition offers forgiveness, but we are often harder on ourselves and find it hard to accept what is offered. With guilt can come a question of restitution. If you find yourself unable to act because of a burden of guilt you might want to think about what you could do to relieve the burden. Writing a letter to the person you hurt—even if you don't finally send it—can help you understand your own feelings and perhaps open the door to accept a measure of grace. Holding back on taking actions in the future because of the burden of guilt is binding and being forgiven or forgiving yourself can be a great relief and can free you to move on with your life.

QUESTIONS FOR STAGE THREE

1. Do you remember a time of being aware of guilt?
2. Can you picture yourself as a child separate from your parents?
3. Did you favor one parent over the other?
4. Did you show initiative at this young age? How so?

STAGE FOUR: INDUSTRY VS. INFERIORITY

> *"This is socially a most decisive stage: since industry involves doing things beside and with others, a first sense of division of labor and of differential opportunity, that is, a sense of technological ethos of a culture."*
> Erik H. Erikson, *Childhood and Society*

Now the child leaves home for the first time. By preschool or first grade, the personality is intact. There is still much to learn, but the emotional energy seems to lessen. The child learns how to work in a group outside the home, take on assignments and complete projects or tasks.

The fourth stage is one of "Industry Vs. Inferiority." For many this is a time when the child fades into the family background. Some have called this a moratorium time when it seems that not a lot is going on.

For me it was an important time. My birthday was just before Christmas and I had just turned six. My brothers and I got up early on Christmas morning. There was some snow on the ground; it was a nearly perfect winter's day outside. We waited at the top of the stairs as long as we could. When the first light of morning had filtered into our bedroom, we could just barely see the Christmas tree and, beneath it, an electric train mounted on a piece of plywood that would be a toy of imagination for many years to come. We would over time build a little town around the track and enjoy hours of play. But when our parents and grandparents had finally gotten up and we finally were able to go down stairs to the tree I made the more important discovery of a full size Schwinn bicycle standing on its own kickstand right beside the tree.

It was more beautiful than anything I could have imagined. The bike was called the Blue Hornet. It had large tires, chrome handlebars, and a tube in the middle of the frame that held a button for the horn. It was first class. Schwinn's brand may have suffered in recent years, but in the 50s it was the best bike available.

In the midst of my excitement, there were sounds of concern. I could hear my mother saying as I came into the room, "That bike is too big for the boy. It will have to go back to the store. Get him something smaller that he can ride."

Granddaddy Billy, who had brought the gift, didn't give in. He held his ground, saying, "Give the kid a chance; let's see what he can do."

I didn't listen long. As soon as I could get my blue jeans on, I pushed the bike out the front door of the parsonage and down the front steps. I got on and rode that bike around the church again and again. I don't have recollection of what it meant to have something exceptional. But I knew this bike was different. The deep blue of the paint, the smell of the new rubber on the tires, the padded seat all spoke of quality in a way that I never experienced before. I was determined to show the grown ups what I was made of, what my Granddaddy Billy saw that was not visible to the others at the time. I didn't feel that I deserved something this nice, but I was determined that I was not going to give it up. I rode that bike almost daily until I left for college some 12 years later. I can still imagine my granddaddy's satisfied smile and his quiet pride.

My bike provided me a means for exploration. My buddies and I would ride the neighborhood on adventures. With the bike, I was free to leave the confines of our yard. We rode downtown to the library and sat on the floor among the bookcases, away from the heat of the summer to read books and dream of even greater adventures. We took tours of different parts of the neighborhood. Once, a neighbor called my mother with stories of our visit to her pond. Some of her fish had died, but we were not responsible and Mother came to our defense. Though at first my bike was my ticket to freedom, later it would become the workhorse for delivering the afternoon newspapers on the route I had for many years. The money from the paper route allowed me to purchase my first of many cars, a 1949 Chevy that expanded the reach of my adventures into teen-age years.

I will never forget that Christmas or the impact of my grandfather and his gift. Granddaddy Billy was bigger than life for me. After the tough times in the late 1920s and 1930s, he came into his own as a salesman for the Charlotte Observer newspapers. He always had a new Chrysler because he traded his car every two years. His cars were like the bike he bought for me: they were first class. The new car smell, soft enveloping seats, big whitewall tires, the fit of the metal and the power of the big engine were all a package. Trading as he did every two years, his car was never old; it was always new and bigger than life for me. When I was little, he would pick me up with his big hands and hold me over his head with great joy. My memory of those days is now in the shadows, but I always knew that he cared for me and was attuned to who I was. With Granddaddy Billy,

I always felt that there would be other chances. I never had any question of his love for me. Like him, that bike became a sustaining symbol in my life, always reminding me of his love and faith in what I could become.

My life changed rather abruptly on Labor Day Weekend when I was ten years old. My grandparents were sitting on their screened-in-front porch with a friend late on a Sunday afternoon. Suddenly, for no reason a car turned off the street, jumped the curb, narrowly missed a big pine tree and headed right toward them. Grandma and her friend ran for the living room; Granddaddy Billy was frozen where he sat. The car slowed and came to a stop right at the brick foundation. No one was hurt and after the initial excitement life resumed its weekend pace, reading the Sunday Charlotte Observer and drinking sweetened ice tea.

Two weeks later my parents were called to come home. Granddaddy Billy had had a heart attack and before they could drive the two hours from our home to the hospital, he was dead. A second heart attack at age 63 in the 1950s was not unusual. It had no doubt been stimulated by the shock to his system, chaos coming from out of nowhere headed toward his seat on the porch. A couple of seconds of drama and our whole family was changed.

Granddaddy Billy came back to his home in a casket. He was laid out in the living room right where he used to recline in his easy chair to read the paper and, in later days, listen to the radio. In the early morning, I stood behind the doorpost of the bedroom watching as my grandma stood silently crying beside him. His booming voice would no longer fill the house. His hands would not raise me to the roof. He often stood between my mother and me when her shouting got out of control.

During this time, my mother's grief overtook her. Because she was beside herself with feeling, it fell to my dad to take care of mother. He harshly told her to stop crying and to get a hold of herself. The message was to be restrained. It was a message I had heard often in my childhood and, while it was directed at her that afternoon, I took it to heart. Life was forever changed.

Grandma insisted that we sing hymns at the service that was held for him. I sat beside her filled with anger that anyone could sing. How could that be? Only now, years later, have I come to understand what that could mean for her and for her hope for a future when they would be joined together. She had buried two children, survived the Great Depression and would live another 40 years. At that moment, she was secure in her faith that this was not an end but a time to lift our voices. Years later I would go to her home for a break from college and would sit across from her at the breakfast table as she served me hot oatmeal and her sermons of simple faith, a combination that held us together in those times when we remembered all that we had lost.

My grandmother was an eternal optimist and believed that she could do anything she wanted. Money should not keep her from whatever she envisioned. The same Grandma who used to read my scribbles as a child and join me in pretending that I was writing also believed that she was a millionaire. When her husband died he left her with a small house that had two apartments in the basement. Two weeks before he had purchased a brand new Chrysler sedan. In those days it was customary to also buy an insurance policy that would pay off the car in the event of your death. Grandma didn't drive, so she sold the paid up car and invested the money. She wasn't a millionaire, but she lived like she could do whatever she wanted!

When it was time for my brothers and me to go to college she believed that we could go wherever we wanted. For me at the time the coveted place to consider was the Lutheran college that was a part of our Southern heritage. So that's where I went. I had no money, so she bought me my first suit and I had a great four years in that college. Between the scholarships and the benefits that accrued to the children of Lutheran clergy my college fees were paid, but it was my Grandma's faith in what was possible that got me there.

So from early on my attitude toward money was rather lackadaisical: what was important was the object of the money, the house, the car, the life style. Once I had an idea about what I wanted, money would be available—persistence was the energy needed to ultimately get there. My grandma taught me how to clean a bathroom and how to dream big.

During the years in Brevard my dad's parents didn't figure much into our relationships. Grandfather Cooper had also died of a heart attack when he was 63, but I was too young to be affected by his death. He had a master's degree in history but had ended up working in the post office in High Point, their hometown. At times he was postmaster, but it must have been a political appointment that you didn't necessary keep. He was a quiet man of few words. He loved to play tennis and, like my other grandfather, I remember him as one who loved me.

I remember a time when he offered me a hard choice. I was spending time in their home and he offered to build a fort for me outside their home or to take me to the movies. Both choices were something I very much wanted, but it could only be one or the other. I remember knowing that I should choose the enduring value, the fort, but that I really wanted to go the movie. I don't remember which choice I made, but I assume that we went to the movie.

My dad's mother was a stern rule setter. She had a nice home with a parlor that no one used and she was a proper lady. She looked down on my mother's family and didn't do much to hide her disdain. I had the feeling from her that I was "too loud" or "too heavy"—that I was too much. My dad's sister did not marry until much later in life and I was like her first child. Clearly she cared for me and neither she nor my Grandmother Cooper approved of my mother. There was always tension in those relationships.

My imagination developed as I learned how to read comic books; soon, I was transporting myself away through elaborate dreams created in my back yard at the base of some big trees. At this point our family was living in a small town that allowed for a lot of freedom for children. Kids would often leave home in the early morning and not return to the house until supper. One summer, I found a large cardboard box in an ally that I dragged home and fashioned into a puppet theater. My friends and I developed a dialogue with plastic figures that were in our toy box and invited our parents to come be the audience for our production. After the summer my dad helped us take the stage to school where we put on the play for our fifth grade class. It was a pseudo-Montessori approach to life.

We were free to follow our interests in the absence of a lot of parental oversight. I remember taking my bag of marbles to school in the early grades. We would draw a circle in the dirt under the stairs of the school and kneel down in the dirt with our thumb and first finger as the grip to hold as we aimed a marble into the circle. We got to keep the ones we could knock out and my collection grew.

My mother did work during some of the summers as a substitute social worker. She came home with stories of her encounters with some of the people up in the mountains—moon shiners and others who received county support. She enjoyed her work and telling the stories. We spent a lot of time at church and in Sunday school, listening to my father's sermons, the liturgy and music.

The life of a pastor's child in the 1950s was quieter and less complicated than the life of a pastor's child might be today. A pastor's child in the mid-twentieth century could still be sheltered from life's ugly side. Clearly for me during this time, I moved through the stage of Industry vs. Inferiority. My bike would take me on adventures and later provide a work vehicle for my paper route. Our neighborhood was safe and we were allowed to move about freely. We had access to books, comics, a radio. School began and it was a positive experience. The experiences of this stage will fold over into the next stage of my life.

By Christmas of the year my grandfather died, my dad decided to take a call, an invitation to start a new church in Austin, Texas. Not only had we lost Granddaddy, now less than four months later we would leave behind the mountains of North Carolina and connections to our extended family to move to a new house and a new city. We were so naïve that my brothers and I believed that we would have to take a covered wagon for the trip. We moved from a 100-year-old wood frame mountain house in a small town to a brand new suburb growing up out of the farmland just outside of Austin. The new houses lined up block after block. We left behind the mountains that were obvious outside our breakfast room to a scraped over piece of dirt that had no trees, not even any grass. That was soon remedied when the builder brought rolls of carpet grass and laid them across the dirt to turn it green. We were all new.

The theory that brought us to this place was built on the idea that ten percent of the population in the United States was Lutheran, so if you built 500 homes and filled them up, you could expect 50 families to show up the next week in the Lutheran box you built on the edge of the community. Dad would walk the neighborhoods inviting people to attend worship in the local elementary school on Sunday mornings. People came and it was not long before a piece of property was purchased and a new church grew out of the ground.

As I look back on that time, I think that I had entered a major depression related to unacknowledged grief. One time soon after my grandfather's death when we were still living in Brevard, my parents left the house for a brief period to go down the street to a bowling alley. I couldn't find them and became hysterical with the anxiety over what would become of us.

After that, I developed an imaginary friend who went with me to Texas. My imaginary friend was someone I could depend on, someone who listened and shared my grief. He and I would ride stick figure horses during recess while the other kids played. The teacher became concerned and contacted my parents. My dad saw some of what was happening and took time to be with me. His ability as a caring pastor and father sustained me through that time in my life. Soon the new neighborhood, another new school and a close friendship with a neighborhood boy gave me enough security that I was able to drop my imaginary friend and come back to real life.

Time can be a great healer and the passage of time

helped me put some of that grief behind me. Still, when the fall comes each year, I catch myself sliding into some sadness and when I remember or remind myself about my grandfather I realize what's going on. It is sixty years later and I am aware of missing him and what he brought to my life.

The stage of Industry vs. Inferiority was an important time in my life. It was complicated by the loss of my grandfather and the move to Texas. But, even with those emotionally powerful disruptions I managed to learn how to do things. I got merit badges and moved toward becoming an Eagle Scout. I was able to do the work required in school and I was learning how to be part of a youth group. While the old issue of shame would return from time to time, it was not overwhelming and didn't move into a feeling of inferiority.

Does Industry Come Easily for You?
Things happen, families move, sometimes families break up. Difficult times affect everyone in the family. But often kids in this time of their lives are becoming more self-sufficient and may appear to those around them as though they are unaffected; they are doing all right on their own. Parents going through difficult times may not have the emotional energy to give to their children especially if the children seem to be doing okay. If you ended up this time in your life with feelings that you were "less than" others— you weren't able to get a school project done or didn't do well with the Girl Scouts—those feelings can follow into adulthood. You might have ended up not knowing how to get started, feeling that you don't have the skills you need faced with a new job or project at work, or unsure

of what's next. You may want to reflect on this time in your life. Taking classes that lead to a finished product, taking up art, photography, training for a half-marathon with a group at the Y—there are a number of ways to fill in the gaps and to observe your own feelings as you enter into these new adventures. There is a great feeling of satisfaction that comes at the end of a race, when you show your first painting, or you share a story you've written.

QUESTIONS FOR STAGE FOUR

1. Were you in the Boy or Girls Scouts? Did you play Soccer or swim on a swim team?
2. Where does your feeling about money come from?
3. Did you have a mentor?
4. What influence did they have on your life?
5. How did your sense of work develop out of this stage of your life?

PART 2

STAGES FIVE AND SIX
WHERE SPIRIT CONTINUES TO DEVELOP

The personality is well formed by this time in life. This next group of stages reflects the maturity of the person into well-defined roles. It is not just the mind that has grown; the interior of the person is becoming more apparent and there will be important decisions made for education, career, marriage, family that will reflect the growing "spirit" of who this person is becoming.

STAGE FIVE: IDENTITY VS. ROLE CONFUSION

> *"With the establishment of a good initial relationship to the world of skills and tools, and with the advent of puberty, childhood proper comes to an end. Youth begins."*
> Erik H. Erikson, *Childhood and Society*

Teen-age years are fraught with conflicting feelings. Now physically filled out, a young person is hopefully succeeding in the educational and social process. What does it mean to be a man or woman? What is one going to become? In this stage we have a chance to rework some of the issues of childhood.

It almost seems that there is a second opportunity extended to us in the years of teenaged turmoil as our personalities take shape. While the core personality is established in early childhood, we now get a chance to rework those issues. Some parents are better parents with teenagers than they were with young children. A child who had a difficult childhood might find a replacement adult in their teens who provides the love and guidance that was missed in the earlier stages. This stage of identity throws everything up in the air as we try to figure out who we are and who we are going to become. From "trust" to "autonomy" to "initiative" there will be opportunities to rework unfinished business. The major concern is getting through this stage alive. There is great risk as the teenager moves out under their own steam—a car wreck, an experiment with drugs or sex gone wrong, family problems or social issues can derail a life or even end a life. As a parent I remember the anxiety and grief I felt as I turned loose of my daughters and they began to find their own way. I knew that it had to happen and I could only hope for the best.

I was not a rebellious preacher's child. In the years that followed I got through junior high and on to high school. I found my way into the Boy Scouts and down the path of the 21 merit badges that led to the Eagle Scout Award. Ironically, given how physically fit I would later become, the Physical Fitness badge was almost my stumbling block—I did not think that I would ever be able to do five pushups. I remember being on summer vacation while I was working on that badge. My parents would put me out of the car and then drive up the road. I would run to the place they parked up the road to get in the required mileage.

Scouts offered an opportunity to join with peers and with our Scoutmaster, Dutch. He was a man who had earned his living as a plumber; he installed water-sprinkling systems in people's yards. But on Monday nights and one or two weekends a month, he was our leader. We learned to work through the requirements of merit badges, to cook bread on an open fire, to sleep in a tent and to hike five miles at a time. We also learned how to make cigarettes out of toilet paper and tree bark and other useful skills. The merit badges added up and were attached to a sash so that when you put on the uniform it was clear how accomplished you were. I was inducted into the Order of the Arrow after spending a night out in the forest with only two matches to start a fire and the expectation that we would find our way back to the main camp without any assistance. Our troop went to a National Jamboree and traded "horny toads" for patches with kids from the north who didn't know any better.

Many years later my oldest daughter was invited to a classmate's investiture service as an Eagle. The ceremony began with an invitation for any Eagles in the audience to join each other in the Eagles' nest at the front of the room and I quickly abandoned my daughter for that fraternity.

As available as my father had been in the early part of our move to Texas, he was generally not around later on. But I had become independent at an early age. By the time I was 11, I had a paper route and over time earned enough to buy that first car, a 1949 Chevy Coupe. I carpeted the inside and added a nice set of Buick hubcaps. I learned how to make basic repairs, tune-ups and always kept the car clean inside and out. Later in high school I added a job at the local drug store on a part-time basis. So I had my own money, bought my own clothes and went where and when I wanted. My parents had a general sense of where I might be at any given time, but much of the time I was on my own.

I remember a time in high school when some friends had decided that we would stay up all night with the intention that we would sneak around and steal hubcaps for our cars. I didn't want to take that risk, but I didn't want to tell my friends. So I asked my dad for his permission to stay out at night. He looked closely at me and then asked if this was a time when he needed to say "no." I nodded and later was able to tell my friends that my dad wouldn't let me spend the night out. When I really needed him he would be there.

My dad was also the one who taught me to drive. When I turned 14, I was eligible to get a driver's license and I couldn't wait. My dad had a new 1957 Ford two-door station wagon that had a Thunderbird V-8. It was a three-speed stick on the column. With all the bravado of a fourteen-year-old, I took the wheel that first time and reached over to turn on the radio. He just as quickly turned it off. Learning how to work the gears and to engage the clutch was not as simple as it looked. Dad was patient, and I learned the particulars about the way the gears were shifted and engaged. According to him, you were not supposed to even feel the gears change.

Over the years since I have had a lot of cars, and many of them have had gears to shift. I always enjoyed it when, after riding with me for a while, a passenger would realize that I was going through the gears, but they hadn't noticed. I was not as successful teaching my daughters in later years as he was teaching me, but I did teach my wife to go through the gears of a new Volkswagen that we purchased in the first year of our marriage. She learned to shift with a grace that would have pleased my dad.

During these adolescent years, I developed a thread that would follow me in life. I enjoyed the position as oldest son in my family, a kid who was active in the local church, Boy Scouts, and choir. I watched my dad work as a pastor. As I matured, I would accompany him on hospital calls and home visits. I was learning at his knee. I have warm memories of opening our gifts at home on Christmas morning when I was older and then leaving to go with him to visit other members' homes to share their Christmas with them. At the time, it seemed like a natural thing to do, but now in retrospect I wonder if was an escape for both of us from an environment that was not as warm or inviting.

Other then the Christmas when Granddaddy Billy had filled our house with nice gifts including that first bicycle, our Christmas gifts were spare, lacking any joy or excitement. I would build up hope that each Christmas would be different only to return after the holidays to hear about the gifts that my peers had received and not having any of my own stories to tell.

I developed a couple of relationships with girls in the neighborhood and then from the high school. My first true love was a young woman I met while working at church camp. During the summers of my years in high school I worked and lived at the camp 100 miles from home. Each week a different group of pastors and their parishioners would come as staff for that particular week of camp. Carolyn was from Corpus Christi and I fell for her completely. She played hard to get and it took a trip to Corpus before the relationship became mutual. We dated from at a distance for a couple of years. She was my date to my high school graduation after-party, but the relationship ended when I left for college out of the state. My parents had come over for the graduation and Mother's comment about Carolyn was that she was too thin and seemed sickly.

I became involved in our church youth group that had local, state and national branches. Church youth groups were often a place where kids who were not popular in school could find a place to be admitted. As the pastor's kid, I was expected to be involved, and I enjoyed the opportunity. The local group met every Sunday evening and we developed our own programs, elected officers, and enjoyed social connections with each other across high school lines. Beyond the local church group there was a state organization that had its own organization and hierarchy.

Early on I had learned that you could enter a new system by being quiet, paying attention, and volunteering for whatever job needed to be done. Just showing up and doing what was needed brought you into the group and in time I was elected to a leadership position. I was the youngest person to be elected president of the state organization. I was a senior in high school, while a college student usually held that position. As part of my post, I traveled the state of Texas visiting other youth groups. I remember as a small child looking through my dad's desk and asking about various medals that he had. He told me that they had come from leading his state organization's youth group when he was in college. I had already back then made a connection between those stories and a direction for the future.

My second experience with death occurred during these years of high school. One of the boys in the church group grew up and left high school to enter the Army. Frank dated one of my friends from Confirmation Class, Charlotte, with whom I had remained friends even though she was some years older than me. When she and Frank began to date, her parents were none too pleased, but they couldn't stop the natural attraction between the young lovers. He was stationed not far from Austin and they were able to maintain their relationship. One night, on his way back to base, he apparently fell asleep at the wheel and hit a bridge railing. He was killed instantly. His death was hard. My dad did the funeral. I sang in the choir. Leaving the church for the cemetery, I was in deep grief, and my mother said something to restrain me, but my dad interrupted her and gave me permission to grieve, in contrast to the restraint he had urged on my mother after her father's death. Frank was too young to die. He had a full life ahead of him. Charlotte and I supported one another in our loss. I remember quite clearly standing in the choir loft wanting to somehow sing the Lord's Prayer during the service, but it was not expected so I did not sing. It was an unrealistic impulse, but the feeling was intense and unexpressed. Even now when I hear the prayer sung I remember Frank and that friendship.

I had different life in the high school. The thread of living in two different worlds was becoming part of who I was. The same skills that served me in the church and at home also were useful in the social community of the large high school I attended. I had a position as a student aide, starting at the bottom and taking on the work that others put aside. In my senior year I joined the high school choir. Learning to read music in the church choir gave me a set of skills that were easily transferred. The choir was a place where I could enter an upper middle class environment that was different from my Lutheran roots. I slipped into that society and learned what was needed to succeed there. I felt like I was part of both groups, yet I was aware of the two lives I had begun to live. I traveled for the church youth group, but I also participated in the social activities of Cotillion and Austin's social group. The two groups were not connected. In the church group I was a leader. I had risen up through the ranks and was one of those who set the tone of the organization. In the high school youth group, I was coming in from the outside. I did not have the economic resources to blend into the environment. I had to learn what the dress code was. I got the required white dinner jacket and the proper tie, learned the dance steps, and dated girls from the group.

During the summers between the years of high school, I worked at our state church's summer camp. For many young church members, spending a week at summer camp was an expectation. The Texas-Louisiana branch of the Lutheran Church had purchased an old pumping station near La Grange, Texas. It was an isolated, somewhat crude place with a group of small houses that the church turned into dorms and corrugated tin showers out back. The main building had been cleared of the big pumps and was now a classroom and dining hall. I was the only full time staff and lifeguard along with the family that lived at the camp. They maintained the buildings and ran the kitchen. Other than guarding the pool and pulling kids out who mistakenly thought they could swim, I mowed lawns on a tractor, taught some of the classes and was called on to kill the occasional copperhead snake that would come too close to camp. Thursday nights we would have a load of watermelons brought in and spend the evening enjoying those fresh cut pieces, playing horseshoes and volleyball.

Each week a different group of pastors would volunteer to come to the camp to be the teachers for the week. I got to watch these men in action and socialize with them during those weeks. I had a night off during each week and I would enjoy borrowing one of the pastor's cars to drive in to town to date some of the local girls. Pastors in that era seemed to enjoy having nice cars and driving them on the long open roads to the Texas hill country. The Best Little Whore House in Texas, called the "Chicken Farm," was located somewhere near La Grange. While I never visited the place it was always fun to say that I would be working in La Grange for the summer.

Around that time I was becoming aware of my leadership skills, moving into the role of President of the Luther League, the activities of scouts, my church, and singing in the school choir all came together in developing a sense of who I was and wanted to become. My dad was a role model as had been my grandfather. I had a lot of freedom, earning my own money, traveling the state for the youth group.

In today's society in the United States childhood and adolescence extend until one is 30 years old. That was not the case in the 1950's and into the 60's. When you finished high school it was an unstated expectation that you were now ready to leave to begin life on your own. That might include going to work in the local factory, joining the armed services or, in a very few cases, going off to college.

I had been making my own spending money since I was 11, I had my driver's license at 14 and my first car at 16. I had grown up without a lot of parental supervision; it was there when I needed it.

So I came to the end of my senior year in high school like most seniors: thinking that I knew everything I needed to know to become an adult. There is nothing like a high school senior for thinking that they have the answers that the world is waiting for. I had graduated from high school; I was working at the church camp for one more summer. I had been admitted to the University of Texas and planned to attend in the fall. I was ready to leave my home and to be on my own—or at least that's the way I felt.

In the middle of my senior year my dad accepted a Call to a parish in Baton Rouge, Louisiana. I could have remained in the Austin community with members of the former church, but I knew even then that I would not be back home after I left for college, so I made the decision to join our family in the move.

Upon reflection I see this period of time as a time when both the challenges and the strengths of my upbringing are clear.

These were hard times for us. My dad had missed being elected Bishop by only a few votes and he was working through what would be next for him. My parents had had a "surprise" baby, my brother Mike, when I was 15. I spent a lot of time taking care of him and we are still close today. My mother was also thrown off by the failure of the election. She lived her life in "reflected glory" as the pastor's wife and had looked forward to being the Bishop's wife. But it was not to be. The move to Baton Rouge was an escape, but not a good one as it turned out. The parsonage we moved into was small, and although there was the promise of a larger one to come, it was still a step down into a community that did not have the flair that Austin had begun to demonstrate even in the early 60s.

My parents fought long into the night. The thin walls of the bedrooms didn't leave much to be imagined; mother's disappointment spilled out in threats to leave and return to North Carolina to her mother's home. While I was not all that excited to have left my friends and community in Austin, I felt that my dad had responded to a Call and that he was where he needed to be, so I supported him and at one point remember telling him to "send her on home," that we would somehow make it without her.

When my parents were in conflict and Mother threatened to leave, I think in that moment I closed the door on my relationship to her emotionally. I was still respectful, but it was not an emotional connection. My experience with my mother convinced me that she would have been happier in work outside our home. Those occasions when she had worked were good ones for her and her role as the pastor's wife was not fulfilling for her. I knew that I wanted a different relationship for my life and early on was not interested in any woman who wanted to be the preacher's wife.

My parents ended up staying through the Civil Rights upheaval in that community. Because Dad was one of the liberal religious leaders in the community, he was wiretapped by the FBI and received other threats to his life and work. Ultimately mother didn't leave him, and they did get a nicer home.

My dad was openly supportive of my activities. He and I played a lot of tennis during my years in high school. I was never able to beat him. He was a powerful competitor, with a blazing serve. But in retrospect I should have been able to wear him down, to finally win. That I could not do that was tied to an undercurrent of disrespect I felt emanating from my mother. I did not want to beat him and add to any insult to who he was. It was never overt, but there was from my mother a feeling of never being satisfied that came to the surface most clearly after Dad's defeat in being elected Bishop and the move to Baton Rogue. Mother's unhappiness became more obvious and my memory of taking my dad's side against her is very clear.

Some of that same feeling of Mother's disappointment fell on me. She did not like the girl that I took to my senior graduation after-party and was open about her feelings. She may have been proud of my accomplishments in high school, but she didn't share those feelings with me. I felt that in some ways she used those successes to add to a put down of my father. I kept my distance from her, but that was not hard because I didn't get a lot of attention from her.

I remember once waiting in my best friend's kitchen before we left for school. His mother was polishing his shoes and it caught my attention. I had no idea that a mother might want to do something like that, something that would support her son in looking and being his best.

I think that my mother's early childhood experiences contributed to a narcissism that was a primary defense for her. She was unable to allow herself to care too deeply for those around her and her dad's early death no doubt supported that need for self-protection. I now wonder if her early experiences of the loss of her younger siblings, the move out of their house and the loss of the family business had not built within my mother a wall of protection against hurt and loss. When her dad died that wall came down for a moment and my dad told her in clear terms to put it back up.

I have come to believe that you have to go back to the foundation, the early history to understand where a person comes from, who they have become, and the end of adolescence is a natural place to make an initial review.

When I think back to my childhood, even though much of those early years aren't available for my memory, I can look back with enough history to understand some of the influences of that time. Having had three children of my own and now five grandchildren I do believe that we come into this world with our own unique personality and that the world engages us and forms us around that basic core. I am clearly extroverted; I am sure that I reached out to those around me. There was lots of available support from extended family and from my parents. I was raised in a safe environment and was fed and clothed in away that would allow me to trust the world. Who I was becoming may have been too much for the world I lived in. The message of putting the lid on, calming down, not getting the "big head" came through. It was not so oppressive that I was prevented from developing a sense of autonomy, but a sense of shame would always be close by.

My grandparents were very positive role models whose lessons have stuck with me all my life. As I look at the way I view money it clearly connects with my grandmother. She paid attention to what she had, she and granddad had installed those two apartments in the basement and she always had a nurse from the local hospital living in the front bedroom. Selling the new car and investing the money provided her a base and she was frugal. I don't think I got too much of the frugal part, but over the years of investing in real estate, fixing up places, starting my own businesses I have been successful. At the same time I often say, "It's only money." When I've wanted to do something and was clear about it, money was not what kept me from succeeding. My granddad's bigger than life personality, his salesmanship have also been an influence. He did not hesitate to seek out the best. His new Chrysler every two years was at the time one of the prestige cars in the U.S. He didn't choose second-class or cheap. The failure of his print shop and the loss of all that he owned did not crush him: he came back, owned his own home, and replaced the lost furniture with antiques that my grandmother liked. I will never be far away from that Christmas when he gave me the bike. Biking has become a major interest of mine, at the same time having good gear is still important to me, and when I have not gotten the best I have usually regretted it.

As important as my grandparents were in my past, my dad was the single most important influence on my life and continues to be. He was willing to work hard for what was important to him. He had integrity and principles that sustained him through out his ministry. I was not aware of his preaching a liberal agenda, but he was liberal in his principles and after I was away from home he stood up for those beliefs in the midst of the civil rights movement. He began his ministry in a time that the church in the U.S. was active and most people attended

Over the years the place of the church changed and he continued on with the model he began, attempting to start churches, keep them running, working at being relevant. His last parish was a success. He took a congregation that had been in trouble and raised their spirit. He helped them build a new sanctuary and retired at a good time, when he was held in high esteem. Two of my brothers followed his course in ministry and had successful careers in ministry over the years. I took a different direction in specialization. But the life of the parish was always important to me. I found there a family that supported me with affection and concern. I wanted him to succeed. Near the end of his life we spent a week visiting together and we left each other in a good place. I felt that I had his blessing and I honored his life and his work. His gentle ability to listen to others and to care for them was always apparent. I was sitting in the hospital when he was preparing for open-heart surgery. As his friends dropped by, most of them clergy, they would begin expressing their concerns for him. In minutes he would be listening to their problems. It was interesting to watch how he turned the agenda away from himself and how appreciated he was.

He would have been a good bishop and he was a good dad.

I am beginning to see that our frequent moves were also challenges for me that I have only begun to examine. I didn't know what death meant when I first experienced it. My Granddaddy Billy, who cared deeply for me and me for him, would never be back, was gone. If you open yourself in caring for and being cared for, you can be hurt when it is no longer available. It became a natural response in my future: when connection is offered you move toward it, but don't let it get too close. At some point you turn away and leave.

We left the community that had cared for us through Granddad's death for a new community. That community welcomed us and five years later we left for Louisiana. My dad was grieving his failure to be elected Bishop, but it was not openly expressed. I knew that I was getting close to a time when I would leave my family, so I went with them, giving up my community in Austin. I would later leave home and not go back.

On the other hand, the Lutheran Church provided a lot of stability. Garrison Keller talks about the Lutheran Church in Lake Woebegone and, while there is a certain reality to his humor, he is talking about a different group of Lutherans. The mid-west Lutherans were a later migration. These people came from the Scandinavian countries: Sweden, Finland, and Denmark. They always struck me as coming out of a certain piety that was not as evident in the German tradition that is part of the Eastern seaboard group.

We were a more pragmatic group, more direct in expression and feeling. There was a real devotion to the local church. Pastors can come and go, but the congregation will hold onto its identity. Some of those mountain churches were known for growing ministers, teaching them the ropes.

As I look back I realize that I was raised in a Lutheran cocoon. We were in church on Sundays most of the day. On Wednesday nights there would often be a supper and program of Bible study. There was the youth group and later the church camp along with the state and national youth group. We had Lutheran colleges and, of course, seminaries. Cradle to grave, you could be Lutheran and not be aware of any other tradition. As will become more clear when I talk about life after college, I had an opportunity for a more expanded view of the world.

The community of the neighborhood and the church were extended family, along with the Boy Scouts and the church youth group, Luther League.

My dad's ministry did not vary that much over the years he served. He moved, met new people, lived in different parts of the South and went through the issues of race and Viet Nam along with the sexual revolution and the ordination of women. But his day-to-day work and life were closely connected to Lutheran past history. Those communities were close and they understood each other. While the churches I would be attached to in the future were different in many ways from my past experience, there has always been a need within me to be connected to that community. I raised my kids in that community, saw them baptized, confirmed, and married there. We buried their mom and my wife from the church. I feel a need for that connection even now.

I had grown up in the family of the church but had never had a direct religious experience. The Christmas Eve service would touch emotions that I did not understand, but I was also beginning to question the reality of the story of the birth of Christ. It seemed otherworldly and while I didn't have words to address what I was feeling I remember the questions beginning to form. I was someone regular on the pew but uninitiated into deep belief. I could listen to the parable of the Prodigal Son and I could identify with the prodigal and with the older son. I knew a father and grandfather like that who was there, waiting for me when I fell down. But I did not have a sense of connection to any God beyond those real fathers in my life. I did not expect to have an answer to prayer or a developed prayer life. I was familiar with scripture but hadn't read the Bible cover to cover. I enjoyed singing in the choir, the experience of blending voices in harmony and of achieving a feeling of participation in the art of music. But I don't remember my dad's sermons. When we went through his things after his death I wanted to have copies of his sermons and I have some. But they are illegible. He clearly worked on expressing his thoughts, but I couldn't follow his outlines. I learned along the way to tune him out and was not moved by his preaching. I could perhaps express some ethical thinking about honesty and respect for others, but I did not learn to think theologically, to see how God was working in my life.

At the same time there was some magical thinking, a need to be in church on Sundays or bad things might happen. I didn't challenge those feelings; I just went to church on Sundays, sang in the choir, connected with my friends and their parents. God was like some kind of secret weapon. I didn't know where he was or how he worked. Things had not gotten so bad that I had had to call on him in a meaningful way. Perhaps that moment standing in the choir loft with the impulse to join the organist in singing the Lord's prayer, or sitting in the pew next to my grandmother wanting to scream at God not sing to the force that had taken my grandfather from me—perhaps those were the closest I came to pushing up against my own beliefs. But I was still laboring under the original rules—to be seen and not heard.

I had come to the end of my adolescence, the stage of Identity vs. Role Confusion. I had survived without making some major mistake. I was ready to leave home to look toward the future. Going off to college is a step along the way, a protected environment to transition from family of origin to a larger family within the community.

There is a concrete sense of having all the answers at age and stage in life. I knew how to work, to earn money, to develop plans and to lead. I had the words of faith that were prescribed by the church and I had not questioned them. I was a person who felt some intense emotions but who had been told in clear terms to suppress those feelings. My grandfather's death left me bereft and angry with nowhere to go with those feelings. Dad had told mother and me, in secondary way, to put a lid on the grief I was feeling. Singing hymns at the funeral did not make sense to me. My later experience with a peer's death would allow for a greater openness to feeling, but not an answer about where God was in that needless death.

Was It Easy or Confusing for You to Create an Identity?

Identity Vs. Role Confusion is a big step in most of our lives. What may have been vague and avoidable now becomes more obvious. Kids come home from their freshman year in college over Thanksgiving and announce to the family that they have discovered for sure that they are gay. When identity becomes the core issue, if you aren't sure who you are, moving into adulthood becomes more difficult. Issues that may not have been addressed in early childhood force themselves to the surface for another effort. It is a time of stress for the child/adult and for those who live and love this emerging person.

This is a big stage in anyone's life. It is a time to rework issues of early childhood, and it is also a time when the physiology of the body is hard at work. Emotions, feelings, and anxiety can be high. It is a time of high risk; an innocent experiment can have a lifelong affect. Many people have families that have high expectations of how their children should act, who they should become or what they should believe. You may now as adult be discovering that you are living out someone else's dream. They may have had the best intent for you, but they did not know the real you. Journaling, meditation, and reflection may help you in listening to the voice within and the sense of who you want to become. It may seem that you have too much invested in the person you are pretending to be to become the person you would like to be. It is never too late to explore that hidden self. You may find that the skills you've developed in one area of your life will bring vitality to the new life you move toward, that you don't lose place but gain wholeness as you become the person you were meant to become.

QUESTIONS FOR STAGE FIVE

1. What were your teenage years like?
2. Did anything like an accident or an unintended pregnancy affect the course of your life during this period of you life?
3. Did you have to put aside dreams or ideas about what you might become?
4. Besides your parents were there other role models and mentors for you during this time in your life?
5. How did your identity emerge during adolescence?

STAGE SIX: INTIMACY VS. ISOLATION

> *"The young adult, emerging from the search for and the insistence on identity, is eager and willing to fuse his identity with that of others."*
> Erik H. Erikson, *Childhood and Society*

Finding one's identity is a fairly narcissistic endeavor. You grow into knowing yourself apart from the original identifiers, no longer a child of the Coopers. You have your own name and sense of yourself. While you carry the family tradition with you, it is an in-between time. Now on your own but still dependent on others and somewhat sheltered, you are free to explore, to become, to learn how to relate to another person, to commit to a future, to take on a working identity.

So it's off to college.

Well, it was not quite that simple. As I mentioned before I had been on the college track in high school. That meant taking Mr. Price's College Prep. English class. The University of Texas was right next door and we all knew that, while the university would admit most applicants, passing freshman English was the way they weeded out who would continue from those who would leave. Mr. Price is one of the few public school teachers whose name I remember. The class was tough and my dad for the first time in a long time came to my aid. Dad was a life long editor and he knew about the requirements of good writing. He would work with my friend Mickey and me on our homework. We learned what we needed to for Mr. Price's class. It was the first time that the direction of high school had some meaning for me. Along with taking the SAT's and filling out the application, I was on my way to the university. I was going to live with one of Dad's former parishioners and there was even the possibility of a better car in the bargain.

That summer after graduation I went for one last time to the summer camp as lifeguard and to a national Luther League Convention in San Francisco. Six of us drove out in the synod's youth director's new Chevy, camping and taking in the sights. There was another pastor's son and four women who were also delegates. It was quite a trip and at end of the summer I was elected to the new national board of the youth group to fill a one-year term. I retuned to our home in Baton Rogue about the same time my parents were returning from their annual trek to North Carolina to re-connect with family and friends there.

While they had been on that trip they visited the college that had hired Dad for a year of fund raising. Lenoir-Rhyne College was a small, liberal arts, Lutheran school located in Hickory, North Carolina, in the foothills of the Smokey Mountains. Their conversations there had turned up the possibility of a scholarship for me at the college. It had never occurred to me to even consider a school other than UT, but here it was a fork in the road. Watching what kids today go through in deciding about which school they will attend and the tension of waiting for an invitation, I, by contrast, only remember it being a given that I would consider college. The one that was offered was the one in the neighborhood. I would like to say that I agonized over the choice, even thought about going to UT, but I cannot say that. My parents were excited about the possibility of Lenore-Rhyne and off I went.

It is amazing to me to sometimes think about what that decision lead me to. Had I gone to the University of Texas my whole life would have taken a different course. I may have ended up in ministry and married, but it would have been completely different from my lived experience.

My trip to the college was symbolic. We lived 1,000 miles from Hickory. It wasn't going to be a day drive for the family to install me in a dorm room. What happened was more typical for my family. A traveling church worker of some sort had stopped by our house on his way to the east coast. My parents seized the opportunity and I soon found myself packing all that I owned in the world into a large cardboard box and the new suit case that had been my graduation present (secured with green stamps). It all fit on the other half of the back seat of a Volkswagen Bug. Off we went on the first of many trips that I would make back and forth.

Having a scholarship did not mean that I would have any money. I had my little savings from the summer and the school provided me a work scholarship. As I mentioned in the first section my family live a clearly established middle class existence, but salary was not the biggest part of that deal. My parents did not own a home until my dad retired. Clergy were the regular beneficiaries of discounts from the members' businesses. I had been used to working for my own money and with this work scholarship my opportunities to earn more were very limited. All through college I would feel that I was broke, and I was. Money didn't stop me from doing things like joining a fraternity or other things that I might want, but that feeling of living on the edge never quite went away. When I unpacked my things at school I had two pairs of jeans—one pair of blue Levi's and a dress up pair of white jeans. Grandmother had sent me with that nice suit from the store where my grandfather had shopped.

North Carolina kids, my peers, were much more clothes-conscious than I had ever been. Every guy wore shirts that had a little cloth hook on the back, penny loafers, and khaki pants. Their shirts were ironed, even starched by their mothers before they arrived, and the dirty ones would go home every two weeks for mom to restore to their stand up quality. Many of my fellow students had grown up in the churches of that area and were connected by their activities in the state youth group.

So there emerged a feeling that I now realize was there in high school: I was an outsider looking in. My connection to Luther League was helpful even there. My election to the national leadership was enough to recommend me as a candidate for president of the class and I was elected. As outside as I felt I started that fall on what would be a political four years at the school. Over time I decided to go out for rush and was admitted into the fraternity for the guys who were not on the football team. It was important to me at the time, but I did not become an active member and by the last year had withdrawn. With no car and with my aunt and grandmother's homes over an hour away I was on campus most of the time. Many of the other students would head home for good Southern cooking and re-connection with their home community. I was there to stay.

I began to date but not very successfully in my own class. It was in the spring that I would meet the woman who would ultimately become my wife. Sandra Greene was a year older and two years ahead of me in our classes. She was the course assistant in a Biology class that I was taking. We flirted a bit around class homework and so it began.

She wasn't sure about dating an underclassman, but we would eat dinner together in the dining hall and the relationship began to grow. I was smitten. But as spring came on she pulled back. The man she was dating had graduated the year before and joined the Army. He was coming to visit and that halted our relationship. I pined away for a couple of weeks thinking that our relationship was over. But after he left we resumed our relationship and by the next year he was out of the picture and we were together from then on.

She was smart and pretty. The first person in her family to go to college, she was the youngest of four kids from a town outside of Charlotte: Belmont, North Carolina. With some significant anxiety I met her parents and was accepted into their family in a close relationship that would continue until her parents died years later.

My in-laws were not wealthy. They would have been considered lower middle-class. They lived in a rented wood frame house near the end of an unpaved street. There were no curbs and cars were parked on the side on the house. The dust from the street left the white wood clapboard looking yellow even after a summer rainstorm.

When you walked through the front door into the living room any impression you had formed on the outside was immediately changed. The living room was warm. It was furnished with good furniture. It didn't hurt that the area where they lived was known for furniture manufacturing, but it was clear that someone had an eye for quality and a sense of taste in color and detail. The center of the room was a long sofa that had a deep green material covering the over stuffed pillows and cushions. The lamps on each end table cast a subtle light through the room and it was immediately inviting and comfortable.

My mother-in-law was an excellent country cook. I was a frequent guest in their home for dinner when I would come down from college to see my fiancée. She had graduated two years ahead of me and had returned home to teach in the local high school. She and her mother worked on making her wedding dress and planning the small ceremony we would have after I graduated and before I would head off to seminary. Her family was most welcoming and I formed a close attachment to her parents that lasted years into our marriage.

After dinner and the conversations that lingered into the night her parents would go to their bedroom and we would settle into that sofa in the living room. It was a close and intimate time in our lives, the foundation of our 46-year marriage. We are often unaware of the backdrop that is the supporting framework of our lives, but when I think of the word sofa, that piece of furniture brings back good memories.

Sandra was as introverted as I was extroverted. I would talk with her about the future or whatever I was studying and she would listen patiently. I remember one conversation in particular. We had begun to trade insults at a point early in our relationships. We were both quick with a quip, but we talked about what we were doing and decided to stop those exchanges.

We had close friendships with other classmates, most of them from her higher class and we enjoyed our time together. She helped me improve my wardrobe and was a helpful editor for my spelling and paper writing. We began making plans for the future. She graduated with a degree in French and went back to her home to teach in the local high school and wait for me to graduate. That summer I went home to work a summer job but returned briefly to participate in a roommate's wedding and took the time to visit another fraternity brother's jewelry stop and to pick a diamond ring.

With great anxiety I proposed that night. I was not surprised that she accepted, but I was relieved and had hope for the future. I promised her a lifetime of adventure, not really knowing what I was talking about, but we would periodically recall that promise. Had she known what that meant she might have given her decision a little more thought.

Her parents were pleased and we began planning a wedding in earnest for the weekend that would follow my graduation. When I returned to my home after that hurried trip, I asked my parents to join me in the living room, pulling them away from the ever-present TV. I told them about the weekend and what I had done. My dad's reaction was immediate: he jumped up from his chair, shook my hand and offered his congratulations. My mother, on the other hand, looked ashen and said, as she got up to leave the room, "You are making a big mistake." She never explained her reaction and I could only speculate that it came out of her frustration with marriage or her feeling that I had not picked someone with wealth or social status. My mother and my wife were never close.

My college years were good ones. I was elected Sophomore Class president and after that I ran unopposed for vice-president and then president of the student body. I was on the debate team, took courses that were interesting and was an active participant in class. Old and New Testament classes introduced me to Biblical criticism and I argued with professors about belief systems. I was majoring in business-economics. It was a solid beginning in business practice, working on balancing spreadsheets and an introduction to the language of business. I took classes in sociology, history, and drama. I was reading widely. I enjoyed being on the debate team. I was not an exceptional student but got by and enjoyed the classes and the interactions.

I worked hard in my year as president to research and introduce a model for an honors program for the college. At first the faculty did not consider the recommendations that came from our student board, but after I graduated one of my professors let me know that the program had been approved, and he thought that it should have been named in my honor. With my grades I probably wouldn't have been eligible to be included in the program, but I enjoyed working on the project and was pleased that it was finally accepted. I enjoyed my college years, was happy to get my degree and I was ready to move on. Sandra and I were married the week after I graduated. Sandra's mother made her dress and one of her students baked the wedding cake. My dad did the service and she and I left for a honeymoon in the mountains of North Carolina, the first of many vacations in those mountains.

I entered Lutheran Theological Southern Seminary in Columbia, South Carolina in the fall and Sandra took a teaching position as a French teacher in a local high school. My time in classes at the seminary fast became the most depressing in my academic career. The faculty had low expectations and seemed to disrespect their students. The faculty were expected to prepare professionals for their life work, but we were treated as novices who did not have any skills and had to be taught the basic lessons of the profession.

One exception was a class called Homiletics, a class on preaching. I did learn some things. We were taught how to write out a sermon in an "oral" style that I still use today. We then preached that sermon to our class and were video taped in the process. The sermon was well received by my classmates and the professor. When I watched the video I was blown away by my hand gestures. My dad had been born with out some of his fingers on each hand and his preaching style included his hand movements. Watching the tape I could see his hands in my gestures. I had internalized his preaching style.

Most of the classes were not that interesting or helpful. It was a depressing time in my life. I was not sure that I was suited for the work but did not see other options for myself at the time. Many of my fellow seminarians were pious, an expression I did not relate to. In other religious traditions it was expected that one had had some direct experience of God picking them out. In the Lutheran tradition it was more subtle than that, but I was not sure that I believed in God, and I certainly hadn't had any sign from above. Also, I felt guilty for not being able to provide for my new wife and myself. I somehow got through basic Greek and finished my first year.

There was another dynamic going on that was harder to recognize. Our country was in the midst of the Viet Nam War and to be in seminary was a way to avoid serving. I didn't agree with the war necessarily, but I wanted to trust the leadership of our country. That became increasingly difficult. Added to that was the beginning of a major change in societal and cultural values. The birth control pill had been invented and in just a few short years we would witness the sexual revolution, along with the assassinations of Dr. Martin Luther King and Bobby Kennedy. The death of President Kennedy had left our nation in a state of grief that still hangs over us.

The fog that gathered around the war and the anticipation of change lay underneath my own lack of direction and the depression that it invited. At this point in my life I did not have a sense of where to go next. I had left home after high school as an unfinished work in progress. I didn't go to college with a goal in mind. It was just the expected next step in my family. I had finished the college prep course in a good high school and so it was off to college. When I finished college I had a couple of suits that my grandmother had bought along with some button down shirts and penny loafers. I also had some experiences in leadership and in becoming an eclectic student. But I did not have a sense of any occupation other than ministry. My grandfather's personality, the hint of a salesman that I watched in him, and my dad's work in the parish were the only models I had for a future.

As summer approached after my first year in seminary I was supposed to join the staff of a local pastor as a summer youth assistant. That pastor took another church and left the area just before summer began. I went on to the church, Mt. Tabor Lutheran Church, and over the summer demonstrated a skill in taking over that was unexpected. I visited people who were shut-in or in the hospital, I wrote sermons and preached. I couldn't administer communion, but I could do whatever else was needed from a pastor. I do remember an anxiety attack that I was able to withstand when I thought I saw a former college professor in the back of the church. I had great respect for him and I knew that he would be able to see right through me. I don't remember if he was in fact there or not. I was able to continue and no one picked up on my anxiety. By the end of summer Mt. Tabor approached the seminary about offering me a job. Of course they were dissuaded.

I returned to another miserable year of classes. That fall I joined two other students in taking on the campus bookstore for a year. It was passed on every year to another group of students, and at the end of that year I walked away with $1,000, a third of what my wife was earning as a public school teacher during those years. We used that "found" money as a down payment on a little brick home for her parents, our first property and one they lived in for the rest of their lives.

It was clear in the first two years of seminary that I was not happy there. But why I was not happy was not clear to me then and is part of the discovery I am seeking as I work through this past history. I had confided my unhappiness to Professor Shell, the professor of Pastoral Care for the seminary. He was also the fieldwork placement coordinator. Our seminary required students to take two years of classes and then to leave the seminary for a year of supervised ministry, usually in a parish somewhere in the United States. It was a mentor/student model, and the learning depended on the place and the teaching pastor. Professor Shell knew from the reports he received what types of opportunities were available. He tried to match up students with the right mentors. Professor Shell had watched me take over the parish in West Columbia where

I had been originally slated to work for a summer under supervision. I had not missed a beat and was soon accepted as the pastor to the parish.

Ministry was not new to me; I had watched my father do the work for years. In the mission churches where he served, his office was often in the house where we lived until a building was secured or purchased. I knew how he worked—I watched him relate to people. On one occasion I took an early morning call from a woman parishioner who said that she was putting her head in the stove and turning on the gas, thinking that she had my dad on the other line. When she hung up, I woke my dad. Somehow I was not shaken by her call. I knew her as a member of the church and responded to her plea for help. We drove to her home and as we pulled into the drive way she entered the kitchen to fulfill her threat. She needed attention, and her call brought what she needed.

It was clear that I did not need to spend another year watching a local pastor work in a congregation. Dr. Shell suggested something else: a new program that specialized in providing hospital ministry and training in crisis ministry. Accredited by a national organization, hospitals hired clinically trained educators to supervise interns and residents in hospital chaplaincy on the same model that was used to hire intern and resident physicians. It was a new movement in the 1960s, and only a few students in our seminary had trained in one of these programs. Later our national church would require at least one semester of training in one of these programs for graduation. I was feeling a certain sense of desperation and I was intrigued by the suggestion. I talked with a friend who was in the class ahead of me and who was in the middle of clinical training in a hospital in Memphis,

Tennessee. He highly recommended the program, and at the same time spoke of its transformative and difficult environment and educational expectation. I decided to apply. The week before I was to interview, Martin Luther King, Jr. was killed in Memphis. My wife and I rode through the South under the cloud of his death and of the curfew that had been imposed across the country as cities erupted in violence and fiery destruction. Memphis, somehow, was spared. I had an excellent interview and was accepted into the fall program.

Still there was the question of my unhappiness with my first years in seminary. In looking recently through the materials I wrote while I participated in the program, I found a third semester evaluation that I had written. I think it provides an important clue:

Discuss what you consider to be the effect of your present training on your future professional performance.

My three quarters of training have had an immeasurable effect on my future professional performance. Formerly I looked at the minister as a weak person with nothing to offer to himself or his congregation. I saw him as a person saying things that no one wanted to hear, leading programs that no one wanted led, demanding money and time from people who did not want to give either. I saw the ministry in the parish as a stepping-stone to synod presidency and some other type of life of value at least the best position available and one that would be the ultimate blow to emulating my father. I am now beginning to see what the minister can really be.

I could not have had a more negative view of the profession I was training for. At some level I knew that I felt this way, but it was too big and too problematic to acknowledge. Everything that defined ministry as an occupation had come from my experience with my dad. How could I feel that negatively about the work and not also have those feelings about him? Yet there they were.

As I look back at that now, I can see what had been happening over some time. When my dad started out in ministry, his first parishes were small ones, followed by two congregations in rural areas of North Carolina. He was bright and energetic; the country was wrapped up in World War II. Childhood surgery on a hip problem had caused him to have a deformed leg that kept him from the Army. He was one of the community leaders; he and the local doctor were the few people in the area with advanced education. Educated clergy were held in high esteem and were sought out for their advice and guidance.

But change was coming and the church and the profession of ministry would be left behind. The other professions of law and medicine became specialized. The incomes and status of those professionals grew. Clergy were general practitioners and there was little career mobility aside from moving to larger congregation. Medicine and psychology became the places to go for issues of ill health, and concerns about contracts and litigation were the purview of the legal profession. Clergy were still called on for ceremonial functions like baptisms, weddings and funerals, but those soon became their main--and only—function. For a while, clergy were the first contact for relationship problems or issues of alcoholism or depression, but they were not trained in treatment options and their only recourse was to make good referrals. Clergy were not even expected to know about running the business of the church; lay boards made those decisions and often did not respect the participation of the clergy in those decisions. Scientific research and thinking was becoming the mainstay of decision-making. The exceptions to all this were clergy like Norman Vincent Peale and Billy Graham, men who led large congregations, had a national following, and advised political figures. There were also courageous civil rights leaders in the clergy like Martin Luther King, Jr. and others in the black community who commanded the attention of the country

But overall, the local pastor was losing ground. Anyone could be ordained—an education was not required and in some denominations was seen as a liability. Clergy were not viewed as decisive forces with public influence. My dad had chosen mission work. He went into a community that had not had a Lutheran congregation and, over time, worked to establish a church, construct a building, and help the congregation reach a level of self-sustaining function. He did not make the transition to the next level of the church's development, building a staff and program. Because of frequent moves, he did not develop a long-term leadership role in the community. He was highly educated and continued to read, study and write sermons, and even edit a state newsletter for the church. The people of his churches for the most part appreciated his pastoral care and his thoughtful sermons. He took a courageous stand in favor of integration that was not popular within one of his churches at the height of the civil rights movement. Failing in an election to the level of Bishop of the church and conflicts in his marriage reduced his effectiveness and in retrospect I see led to some depression. His sermons took on an angrier tone, and he withdrew into his reading and work as an editor. I loved and respected him and wanted more than anything for him to succeed. His was my role model and I needed to see a future that had hope. I was caught in an internal conflict. Holding up my father on one side and, on the other, knowing that his model was failing, I did not know what to do, where to turn.

Meeting Robert Lantz became the answer to my conflict and to my future. Bob Lantz was also a Lutheran clergy. I had never interviewed for a position and the supervisor Bob Lantz was an intense to the point of austere man who asked penetrating questions and listened deeply to the answers. I was drawn in and felt that this man had an internal sense of his own authority that I had not experienced in other people. I was accepted into the program along with four other seminarians and in the fall began an intense program of crisis chaplaincy and written introspection.

Sandra and I moved into an apartment that we found in inner city Memphis. My stipend at the hospital included meals at the hospital. Sandra secured a position as a French teacher in an exclusive Episcopal girls school so we lived with the extreme contrasts between the poverty of an inner city hospital and the suburbs and isolated luxury of young women who lived in the suburbs.

We discovered over the fall that there was another couple in our building, newly married and getting started in their lives. The husband was an African American man who worked at Baptist Hospital; his wife was a blond white woman whose father was the president of a large corporation. In 1968 their relationship was not usual. We became good friends. We played golf on the city course in the months that followed. While we did not maintain the relationship after we left Memphis, our lives would touch again in the future in unexpected ways.

A pattern that was beginning to emerge was the separation between what was going on in my work and what was happening at home. It had begun in seminary. There had been little to report to Sandra from my classes or experiences. We enjoyed our few friendships, going to movies and out to dinner occasionally. Later we would acquire a large tent that would allow us to make trips to the beach or to the mountains until we were in a position to afford a Holiday Inn. Seminary lectures were not relevant to life as we knew it. That same pattern carried over into our lives in Memphis though for different reasons.

Memphis City Hospital was joined with other smaller hospitals in the inner city of that town by the Mississippi River. The buildings were a mixture of old and new. I worked in wards that included 35 beds in one large room separated by curtains hanging from the high ceiling. But I was also connected to a new unit that had a number of dialysis machines and patients spending hours watching their blood wash through these machines that removed the toxins and allowed them to live, maybe even work when they left the room for the outside world. I worked with patients who wanted to talk about their lives. Coming to the hospital even for a non-life threatening treatment alerts a person to the fragility of life. Giving up your clothes, billfold, credit cards, for a gown that doesn't tie, finding yourself flat on your back looking up at the people who enter your room or come to your bed side is a regressive experience. You begin to get some hint that you may not always be in charge of where your life is taking you. At those moments having someone available to simply listen to you can have significant value.

I heard stories about people's lives and began to see patterns between physical sickness and emotional life experiences. Our new supervisor emphasized that as Chaplain Interns we were on the same level as the Medical Interns: we received the same salary and were a part of the professional staff. The late 60s were a time when technology was entering the medical field in a bigger way. There were now treatments and medicines that could provide cures that had not been available before. I watched open heart surgery being performed for the first time in the city. I listened as doctors made decisions about who would be able to receive the limited services of dialysis, the difference between life and death. There were connections to cancer and grief and to heart problems and stress that were just beginning to be acknowledged. In the past the hospital had been the place you went when you were sick and did not have a home to go to. Now the hospital was becoming the place to go for treatment and ultimately the place to die. When everything else failed it was time to call the "black shirts," the clergy. We were there to stand with the patients, families, and staff when science had run its course and it was time for the spirit to take over.

The new training model was completely different from anything I had ever experienced. We met each morning as a group for an hour and a half seminar. The supervisor, Bob, sat at the head of the table the five of us gathered around. Each day one of us would present a verbatim.

This paper had grown out of the training of social workers. It consisted of three parts: an introduction that spelled out what was known before a visit occurred in some detail and the reason for the visit. The introduction was followed by a rendition of the conversation that the visit contained. It was an attempt to record what the patient said and the response of the chaplain. The final section was an analysis of what had occurred. Why was this visit selected? What were the underlying issues? How could the visit be improved? What did the relationship say about the chaplain's own emotions?

It quickly became obvious that the choice of the visit, the remembered conversation, the analysis, were all potential pathways into the interior feelings, emotions and unconscious of the chaplain. While there was some interest in the patient, the focus of the discussion was more on the practitioner. Each day one of us presented and the attention would focus on that chaplain. The sessions were intense and revealing. Our group grew in their trust of one another, and the content of the verbatim increased in quality and length. When we actually recorded a visit and transcribed and then compared it to the remembered account we saw immediately that what was remembered was a small part of the actual visit, but what the chaplain remembered was what was important. We were learning from experience.

I would later read about transference or developmental stages, about ego, id, and super-ego. But in these seminars we were experiencing first hand what counter-transference was. We were looking at our relationship to one another and discovering how much we were alike and not alike, what our childhood experiences had meant in our character development. Again the theory of adult learning would give content to the experience, but for the time being I was learning how to learn from experience. In addition to the daily sessions we each had an hour during the week of individual supervision or therapy. These too were intense sessions. Bob could listen thoughtfully in a way that invited me to trust him and to open myself up to him in a way that I had never thought of on my own or had shared with another person. I began to understand my depression. I realized that I had spent much of my life day dreaming, reading fiction as an escape, thinking about the past, dreaming about the future. I began to live more in the moment, to think more about my interests and my capacity. I took risks in expressing myself both in the seminars and with Bob as well as with the staff and patients of the hospital. I entered into significant relationships with patients.

For instance I had become close to an older man who had emphysema. He was now reduced to living in the hospital on a more or less permanent basis. In the course of his time in the hospital he was offered a new series of drugs that had an immediate and significant impact to his shortness of breath. He was delighted and hopeful and we talked about what he might do if he left the hospital. Then the drugs began to fail and it was clear that he was reverting to his earlier difficulty. I had visited in the afternoon and we talked about his disappointment. Later that night my wife and I were watching the evening news when a report came on about a man who had walked out of the hospital and into the nearby Mississippi River and drowned. That man was my patient. I grieved for him, but also understood what that final act of courage and effort that meant to him.

I was assigned a long-term counselee. A previous intern had seen her for a year and she was passed on to me. We met weekly for an hour of therapy and I recorded each of our sessions. My verbatim on those visits gave me great insight to my relationship with my mother in particular and to women in general. I think I was of some supportive help to her, but I know that she was a great teacher for me.

That year of training was transformative for me. Learning took on a whole new meaning. Theory and content were no less important, but I now sought out the theory to better understand what I was experiencing. Our supervisor would guide us into deeper waters of understanding how our feelings and emotions were affecting our self-definition and our work. At the same time he modeled a different behavior for a clergy professional. He dressed professionally; his clothes and shoes were the very best. He drove a new Mustang, had a large powerboat on a local lake and lived in a nice apartment near the hospital. He read the Wall Street Journal and advised us on investments and long term financial planning. He had respect for our educations and asked us to demonstrate our skills in our work with patients and staff. It was my first introduction to the concept of Adult Education, on the model of John Dewey: learning from experience. We would immerse ourselves in the work, step back to write reflections on that work, research what we did not understand, and then return to the work with informed ways of working. After the initial adjustment to the new system, I found the work to be exciting and life giving. Our supervisor was a clergy worthy of respect who was teaching me how to earn my living by providing a valuable service to others. He was a man of personal and professional authority who was not afraid to be successful on both personal and professional levels. After having arrived in Memphis as a depressed student driving a Volkswagen; I left a year later in a brand new Oldsmobile hardtop with hope for my future and hard questions for the professors of the seminary that I was returning to. It was the beginning of a long-term career in teaching and providing therapy and leadership within the not-for-profit community.

When I retuned to seminary in the fall of that year I went back with a whole new attitude. I wrote a paper on medical ethics, and I found a part-time position in a local church. I sought out my professors for conversations about the profession. My depression had begun to lift and I had newfound energy a sense of direction. I now felt some sense of call to ministry, to becoming a clinical teacher and therapist. It was an exciting year and I was a real student for the first time in 18 years of classroom experience.

Up to this point I have talked about my vocation and my belief in God in terms of what I wasn't. I was not a pietistic person or pastor-to-be. Yet I felt that there was more to life than a surface day-to-day existence. The Lutheran tradition spoke of grace as a gift, not something to be earned. I resonated with that belief. I believed that the scriptures provided insight into living and that there was a creative spirit alive in the world. I did not feel that God was in control; more that I was created uniquely and was in a process of discovering who I was and what my purpose or call was to be. I entered the process of clinical training and began to discover psychotherapy, the collective unconscious, and the insights of the analytic process and was able to merge them with my role as a clergy. Up to this point in my life I had been swept along by my position in my family, and by the various opportunities that had come to me. But I did not feel that I had necessarily chosen that direction. I ended up at Lenoir-Rhyne because my family had good feelings about that school. I went to seminary because no one had suggested another possibility. Given my enjoyment of the politics of student government one might assume that thinking about becoming a lawyer might have come up. It didn't and I ended up studying Greek and having classes that did not have much meaning for me or for life as I knew. When I was finishing at the seminary I had one final committee to meet before being authorized for ordination. At the end of an energized meeting with that group of mature pastors one of them asked me "Do you believe in God?" I paused for a moment and answered, "Most of the time." That answer summed it up for me, the committee passed me without more discussion and that answer would still be the one I would give if I were asked again.

I had successfully finished college, I had met and developed a long-term relationship with a woman and we were married. That was a choice I made. At the same time neither one of us really knew who we were or what we would grow to become. We shared similar values and backgrounds and we held on to each other in our aloneness. We shared similar religious values. For me I had grown up in the church and had a certain pragmatic view of the church as a human institution. Sandra's family had been members of the church but not enrolled in the inner workings of the church. She had benefited greatly by the support of her teachers in school and by the support of the church youth group and pastor. But she was more afraid of religion and was cautious about the possibility that expressions of faith could get out of control. While her parents were very accepting of me, Sandra's dad could not believe that he was going to have a son-in-law who was a clergy. It was a joke that we shared with each other.

I would learn later about the abusive environment that Sandra had grown up in. As the youngest child she was able to avoid some of the most painful teasing and hurtful comments. As our own children would later join our family I found myself standing between my children and

Mr. Greene's hostility. He treated his other grandchildren with disdain, but he knew better than to bring that mean spirit to my children.

So I returned to seminary with a new view of ministry. I could see the value in feelings and in trying to understand human behavior. I felt that the church could provide a healthy community of support for people and that the pastor could be a significant therapeutic leader in people's lives. The rituals of the church gave meaning and purpose to life transitions and I was excited about the future.

One of the books I was introduced to in my return to seminary was called *The Church In The Way*. The thesis of the book was that church could be a place where people could try on different behaviors and develop new skills in a non-threatening environment. A person could learn how to sing, even read music, could practice skills as a teacher or youth leader. The farmer or store clerk could sit on the board and learn business skills. The church could provide a supportive environment for personal growth and could be there where people faced illness, problems with their children, marriage concerns, death, the significant times in their lives. I developed a plan for my future around that book's theory and my experience in clinical training. I began to prepare for ordination and for a call to a parish.

In the Lutheran tradition in order to be ordained one had to have a call. For a new graduate from seminary the call had to come from a congregation. Graduate school and specialized ministry could only be considered after spending three years in a parish.

Christmas of my senior year, Sandra and I joined her family for a long drive to Miami, Florida. Her grandmother was not doing well and we joined her parents in the drive.

For a number of reasons it was a terrible trip. On the way home that we bummed with some friends I said to anyone who would listen that I would "never" go back to Miami; it was that bad. As the winter thawed and the search for a first call to a parish began I listed my first choice as a location anywhere in Virginia. I liked the Bishop there and my mentor had moved to Annapolis so that without too much trouble I would be able to maintain a connection to his wisdom. I was invited to several churches, but none of them felt right. Then two invitations came together, one to a position as Associate Pastor at a large church in Springfield, Virginia. It seemed to offer everything I was looking for, and it was only an hour from Bob's new location in Annapolis. The second call came from a senior pastor in Miami! One of my peers had recommended me to this man who had a reputation as a great preacher and a real character. He called me from party at a parishioner's home and invited me to come for a visit.

Remember I was "never" going to Miami again in this lifetime. Sure enough we got on that plane and the interview went very well. The next week I interviewed in Springfield with a seasoned pastor who was well organized and would no doubt have been a good teacher. But he lacked the creative edge that Carsten Ludder offered. It was part of the adventure in life that I had offered my wife when I invited her to marry me. I ended up driving a yellow 914 Porsche, playing golf on the best courses Miami had to offer and learning how to write and deliver sermons from one of the best in the field. It was a heady three years and the right choice.

I also discovered again how much I enjoyed the parish. I became the pastor to a growing community in South Miami, visited them in the hospital, in their homes, at their work.

It was typical of a first call for a young clergy fresh out of seminary and his wife. The older adults of the congregation adopted us. We were invited to their parties and often had dinners with them in their homes or local restaurants.

I was also learning from Carsten about the work of sermon development. Everything he did, everyone he met, and every experience he had could be possible food for a sermon. He would begin in the fall outlining the scripture lessons for the next year's sermons and would begin looking for illustrations. He frequented the latest movies, and sought out people of interest for conversations. He was constantly looking at his experiences through the eyes of the upcoming text. His sermons were well written and he could hold the attention of the congregation for 30 minutes without a problem. He often said that he had only "one" talent and he used it to the hilt.

We began to develop a good friendship. He would spend hours after Sunday's service or after meetings at church talking about his past and I was learning from him about the work of ministry, not unlike my experience in clinical training. I sought out a therapist to continue working on my own self-understanding. Sandra was unable to find work as a French teacher and ended up in some part time positions. For the most part we enjoyed the casual life style that Miami offered and the friendships we developed.

But I had committed myself to continued training and as the end of the required three years approached I begin to apply for residencies in clinical pastoral education. After Christmas that third year I interviewed in Baltimore, Richmond and Atlanta and was offered positions in each program. Richmond was my choice because it had been the site of my mentor's training experience and the primary supervisor, Pat Prest, was well known in the history of this relatively new movement. Pat could generate a transference, father/son relationship in an instant and I felt drawn to MCV and to the training model there. The other faculty was also impressive. Luther Mauney was a distant relative and a Lutheran pastor that I had been introduced to in my college years. He was very bright and a good role model for me. He later became a best friend. Roy Woodruff had a Ph.D. in pastoral care and had been brought to the university to develop a degree program in pastoral care. I accepted their offer and prepared to leave Miami.

Carsten was not pleased that I was leaving. On hearing the news his initial response was to say that we would not want to tell anyone until late spring about my decision. The next Sunday he announced to the congregation that I would be leaving. I wondered how it would be to hang around for seven months after the announcement. I discovered that it actually was a good decision. I was able to help recruit my replacement and orient him to the parish, and I found that once people knew that I would be leaving the intimacy of our relationships deepened. In the years that have followed I took full advantage of the time to develop those relationships.

The church didn't want me to leave and I was ambivalent, but I felt that it was the right choice. The president of the church council suggested that if I would just stay that they would replace my 914 Porsche with a 911. He knew how to tempt me. I loved working in the parish and I continued throughout my career to find lasting relationships in the various churches we joined in each of the communities we moved into. Many of my professional peers had not succeeded in the parish and had sought out specialized work as a way to be in the profession but not connected to a congregation. That was not the case for me and I would later on two occasions attempt to bring clinical training into the congregation rather than the reverse.

We successfully moved to Richmond and Sandra was able to find work in a local high school as a French teacher. We were set for the two years of residency. But the Medical College of Virginia's training program could not have been more different from my experience in Memphis. Beginning in the fall another new student and I joined an already formed peer group of men and one woman. My expectation that the teachers would all be like Bob Lantz proved to be mistaken. I expected more time of self-reflection and soon discovered that I was not in touch with my feelings and was not holding my own in the training group. I had been used to succeeding on the basis of relationships and that model worked in the hospital and elsewhere but not in this group that expected me to be able to listen to my feelings and use them in relationship with my peers and supervisors.

Carsten invited me to return to Miami to preach the morning service on Christmas Eve. He felt that I would draw a crowd who would come back for Christmas Eve. It was a heady experience, in contrast to the feeling of failure that I was experiencing in the training group. Soon after I returned I was expected to meet a committee of local clinical educators who would pass on my readiness to begin preparing to teach on my own. I failed that committee badly—so much so that I literally could not find my way home for almost an hour after leaving the meeting. I had never experienced failure like that before and it opened up my issues of narcissism and ultimately opened me up to enter the training I would need to become a successful teacher. But at that moment in time I didn't know if I would be able to remain in the program. I was put back a level in the training group and I spent that semester and the summer working in therapy and in my new peer group. It was a painful experience but one that opened me up to the world of my emotions and a better understanding of what I was feeling in the moment.

At the same time I had been supplying a vacant congregation in Northern Virginia, a promising parish in an affluent area that was growing. It was an ideal congregation and they were making every effort to entice me to leave MCV and to become their pastor. I resisted and continued my work in the training program. I worked for three years as chaplain to the alcohol detox program in the hospital and developed a paper on that work that opened the door for me to re-enter the supervisory training program. It was not without its moments, but over all I began to succeed and was finally given a chance to have my own group of students. When I wrote up my work and presented to a regional committee of supervisors I was affirmed in the work and endorsed to begin to look for a training program of my own.

I worked through the rest of that third year and another summer group and left that experience as an Acting Supervisor of Clinical Pastoral Education and as a Member of the American Association of Pastoral Counselors. I began a life long love of putting theory to work in understanding practice and I began to fully live into the idea that I could approach anxious places and people as opportunities to learn rather than as something to avoid or contain.

One of the advantages of being a young married, childless couple meant that as a graduate student I could devote my full time to my education and experience. In addition to the training I was getting as an educator, I also paid for supervision of my work as a therapist. The local pastoral counseling center in town the Virginia Institute of Pastoral Care (VIPCare) had their own training program and I joined them for supervision of my work with clients and later co-led a group with a seasoned therapist. When I finished at MCV I had met another group of certifying practitioners who reviewed my tapes and write-up of my work with a long-term client. They voted to endorse me at the first level of membership in the American Association of Pastoral Counselors.

So it was time to move on. The stage of "Intimacy Vs. Isolation" had been confronted head on. I had entered into marriage and had chosen a profession. Initially I had been moved along by parental and societal pressures, but as I moved into clinical training and my last year of seminary I had come to a place of self-understanding that allowed me to make choices for myself and my future. I wanted to locate in Virginia for my first call, but Miami was the place that offered the best place to continue learning. I enjoyed the parish and was encouraged to stay but I chose to continue the process of training and specialization. In the midst of the hard times in the training experience an attractive parish that could have been a career parish courted me, but I chose to remain in Richmond and to press on toward my goal. All of that to me represents the issue of intimacy. I was clarifying my identity and choosing my professional role in life. To commit to a role or a relationship is to become intimate, to know and be known both by my wife and by my professional associates.

From a theological perspective I have come to a place of hearing Jesus' primary message as one of the "Kingdom of God is now." That translates for me as living in this moment, honoring the past and acknowledging the good and not so good that is part of that past, but not living back there. At the same time we hope for the future but don't live in that place. As I listen to Jesus being revealed in the Gospels of Matthew, Mark and Luke I see him evolving into the man he becomes. Jesus is a true man and is self-aware and at the same time becoming. His life and ministry is a living growing experience with hope for a future that is not realized for him but perhaps over time is beginning to be understood. The same "saved by grace alone apart from works of the law" that Paul writes about and that Luther discovered becomes the hallmark for taking up life's adventure. What our culture and parents taught us is part of who we are—the past—but not who we will become—the future. What we have is who we are right now in this moment, growing in our knowledge of who we are and in our ability to commit to who we are becoming.

Is Intimacy Your Go-to?
Or Do You Tend Toward Isolation?

This stage is closely linked to the stage before it. If you are unsure of who you are, it is going to be hard to commit to another person. As you grow into knowing who you are, it is not unusual to outgrow childhood relationships and to move toward new connections. Intimacy is the ability to share fully of yourself with others, not just through a physical connection but with a sense of revealing your true feelings and your own unique view of the world to others. People who immerse themselves in their family and their work may find that they are discovering their capacity for intimacy, sharing with others and themselves the truth about who they are and how they see life. There will always be the fear of failure, the pain of losing a connection, but often people discover that hard times were also times when they were most alive and when they learned most about themselves. Find a trusted therapist you can talk to, a mentor, a role model that you can learn from, read widely about how others handle life and take the risk. It will be worth it.

This stage of Intimacy Vs. Isolation is now delayed into the late 20s. You can be an adolescent until you are 30. After that you have to grow up. Clearly it was a busy time in my life and decisions that I made during this time continue to be part of who I am today.

QUESTIONS FOR STAGE SIX

1. Did you go to college or into the military or some other type of sheltered initial experience when first leaving? What impact did that have on your life?
2. Intimacy is more that physical closeness. It includes a deeper sharing of your inner-self. Did you have experiences with others that allowed them to know you at a deeper level?
3. Was the transition from home an easy one or one filled trial and error?
4. Any regrets?
5. Did you discover a direction for your life and/or career?
6. Did you have a mentor and how did that work for you?
7. Were there some difficult choices, mistakes along the way?
8. What did you learn about yourself in the process?

PART 2

STAGES SEVEN AND EIGHT— THE TIME OF THE BODY

So now that you are who you are, Erikson's last two stages are ones with long periods of time hopefully as you work though the big issues of life, marriage, family, and career and into retirement. The tension is between staying active and falling into habitual behaviors that no longer have their initial energy. It becomes increasingly clear that your health becomes a determining factor. Without good health you have other challenges to face and the quality of life can be diminished. We become aware of our bodies in new ways, what may have been a focus on looks in the past and was taken for granted, now starts to have new meaning. You may have a "bucket list" but without health checking off some of those postponed goals may be a problem.

STAGE SEVEN: GENERATIVITY VS. STAGNATION

> *"Generativity encompasses the evolutionary development which has made man the teaching, and instituting as well as the learning animal."*
> Erik H. Erikson, *Childhood and Society*

It's now time to enter the work of adulthood. We have the "tickets" that we need to follow our profession, and we have our first real job in our chosen profession. We are settling into a community, developing friendships, and finding outlets for other interests. Erikson speaks of this long period of time as one of Generatively Vs. Stagnation. How does one keep growing, learning becomes the challenge? Life can become a routine or continue to be an adventure.

I entered my 30s and was ready to enter fully into becoming a professional clergy and family man.

My residency was ending. I had secured my initial credentials. As an acting supervisor in the Association of Clinical Pastoral Education I had the endorsement to go out on my own, to start my own program. I could also apply at other institutions that were training clergy. As a member in the American Association of Pastoral Counseling I could see clients for therapy while continuing to consult on my work. I was board certified to go to work as a specialized clergy.

In the spring of 1975 I began the job search. I wanted to stay in Richmond. We liked living here, and we had purchased an old duplex in the city and had been repairing and fixing it up. We rented the down stairs while we lived upstairs. Once we had finished the upgrades we moved downstairs and rented the upper unit. Sandra had a good job teaching French. We were active members in a local church and had good friends in the community.

Initially there were no openings at the hospital where I was training. I went to work and wrote a grant to fund a position for the chaplain's role in the detox unit that I had served for three years and I waited for the results. I also applied to the Virginia Institute of Pastoral Care (VIPCare) where I had been paying for supervision of my work as a therapist. They did not have any openings and did not expect to expand. So I began to look beyond Richmond. I was preparing to teach another unit of Clinical Training that summer and did not have a lot of time to pursue the job search.

As it turned out the grant came through in the late spring, so that it was possible that I could have become the chaplain to the Alcohol and Drug Treatment Center. At the same time one of the staff at VIPCare decided to move out of their one CPE slot and I interviewed for his position. The interview went well and I was offered a position as a therapist and as a clinical instructor. I would run a Community Center in one of the poorer communities of Richmond, developing a Clinical Pastoral Education training unit in that center. Needless to say I went into the summer with a sense of relief and excitement about the work ahead.

Ideally work provides the place for being generative. But that is not always the case. The first time you go through tax season as an accountant there is a lot to learn. The second year might not be quite as exciting and by the third year you know what is expected. Unless there is continuous opportunity to grow and change a person could be stuck doing the work but becoming stagnant. In the history of work in the United States a person was expected to seek out a career job with a company and to stay with that company for the next 30 or 40 years until retirement. The company would provide for your health care insurance and for retirement. All that was to change abruptly in the 1980's. But at this point in my life the model for one's life work was laid out clearly.

The Executive Director of VIPCare in making his offer said that I could do anything that I wanted to do as long as it was ethical and in keeping with the agency's charter. I felt a great deal of freedom.

I set about establishing a community-based unit of clinical training while I oversaw the daily operation of the center. That summer I had five students enrolled in a creative unit of training outside the hospital context. Five seminarians formed the training group. Each was assigned to one of the congregations in the community including the Catholic Church. Each student was also assigned to a community agency like the mental health clinic where they were expected to develop a connection. We also had clients and programs at the community center for their involvement. The students were engaged in the life of the inner city. For instance one student connected with one of our neighbors. When that neighbor developed a health problem and ended up in the hospital, the student visited there and followed up when they came home. It was unique training for seminarians. Our seminars shared verbatim from a variety of settings and experience, so students learned not only from their own experience but also from the experience of others. It was experimental but utilized the educational philosophy of the movement and as such had integrity.

Unfortunately for various reasons the center was not able to fund the contract after the summer ended. I left the center and moved into full time work as a therapist at VIPCare. I wrote up the summer's experience along with all the tapes of the sessions and applied to meet the national certifying committee of the Association. The supervisors of the area, the very ones who had turned me down in my first committee meeting, did not hold out much hope that I could present a unit that was so radically different from the usual and be fully certified. It was worth a try and I didn't have another place to do clinical training in the foreseeable future. In January Sandra and I traveled to Chicago for a very enjoyable weekend and on Monday morning I met the national certifying committee. My approval was unanimous! From my initial introduction to the clinical model in Memphis to my near failure with the model in Richmond, I had emerged with the tickets to have my own training program. It had been a long, hard road.

In the years that followed I went on to finish the ultimate certification as a pastoral counselor and complete a Doctorate of Ministry in Pastoral Counseling at Union Seminary. It was an exhausting experience, so much so that when I finished the month of comprehensive exams required by the seminary I left the testing area for the doctor's office and ended up in the hospital for a week with pneumonia.

I had moved up in the VIPCare leadership structure to Director of Training, a vice-president's position, and I was managing a full caseload of clients and overseeing a training program for pastoral counselors. My work as a therapist was growing and I was becoming more skillful in the work. I had clients who came individually, some for as long as three years. Others moved from individual work into a regular group that I co-led with another therapist. It was very satisfying to watch people move from anxiety and dysfunction into more successful ways of relating the world. In the hospital I had worked with alcoholics who were at various stages in the process of becoming sober. In my clinical practice at VIPCare I often saw people who had been the spouse of or child of an alcoholic and could see first hand the difficulties that addiction had brought to the family and the individual.

As the Director of Education for the agency I developed a training program that was ultimately accredited by both the Association of Clinical Pastoral Education and by the American Association of Pastoral Counselors. We had a group of advanced residents who worked right along with our staff therapist and were supervised in their work with clients. Two of those residents and I developed a research project around issues of communication between couples who came to us for therapy. We would each develop verbatim of our work with a couple, taking it to a case study level. In our study group we would then look at the themes that emerged and from those case studies we developed an article pointing to the need for couples to have a common understanding of the dream for their family. Many people had begun the marriages with hope for a future that did not materialize and without a shared hope for the future there seemed to be little hope for the marriage. It was exciting work and we could see benefit to our work with couples in the process.

That research explored theory that I brought home and into our marriage. Initially Sandra and I had not been sure that we wanted to have children. We both enjoyed our work and our free time. We had not come from extended families with extra wealth or energy to support us in the beginning. There were significant changes beginning to occur in this time frame. With the development of the birth control pill couples had a freedom to decide about having children. We had initially decided that we would not have children. Again my mentor, Bob Lantz, had made that decision with his wife and while he did not directly recommend that pathway his model was a powerful one for my wife and me. But entering our 30s we began to re-evaluate those choices and decided to have a child.

It was a very intentional decision, but like the idea of having a life of adventure, having children is not something you can anticipate with clarity. Jennifer Lynn was born nine months later and we both were completely taken with her, so much so that two years later we decided to try again. This time to our surprise the next child turned out to be twins, Katherine Anne and Laura Anne. We discovered that more twins are born to women who are 38 than at any other time in their lives. Sandra was 38 and she was in shock. From the first announcement of the pregnancy I was excited. Of course now nothing worked. We had everything we needed for a second child and now we needed everything again for the third child: car seat, bed, a larger car. The income we had enjoyed as a working couple was not going to stretch to three children in childcare. I was also at a stalemate at work.

Even before the twins were born I had begun to think of leaving VIPCare to start my own counseling office. Bob Lantz had opened an institute in Annapolis and I thought about fashioning my own organization along the lines he had set down.

I was growing in professional experience and knowledge. When the executive director stepped down, I considered applying for the director position, but there was another man who had been there longer and I deferred to him. Over time, I grew to regret that decision. He was a caring man who worked hard and expected the same of his staff, but he could not make a decision. He would labor for months about approving a new program or direction, his desk piled up with paperwork, and the staff was beginning to lose respect for his efforts.

I found myself coming home with headaches, a problem that I had never had before. I knew that a change was necessary. I had a good solid client base by this time and a reputation in the community for my work and leadership. I had begun to look for offices and to develop a business plan to open my own office perhaps with a partner.

Then came the news of the twins and among all the other changes that implied it put the idea of going out on my own onto the back burner. Our oldest child was in pre-school. The twins would need to be in daycare if my wife continued to teach and the income from her teaching and the costs of daycare would be close to a wash. We did not have family in the area; we were on our own. Sandra's parents were older and travel to Virginia was a hard trip for them both physically and emotionally. We were living in a different world economically from the one they knew. They did not begrudge us our life style, but they didn't understand or feel at home in our home.

My parents on the other hand did come to visit, but as my mother walked into the breezeway entrance to the house she said, "I don't do diapers anymore." I looked at her and responded: "Then why did you come?"

Living in Richmond we were surrounded by the ultimate in Southern family traditions that included the custom of "all hands of deck" when a new baby emerged. All the relatives would show up and the women would take over with advice and real help. But our families weren't there. We were an island of two people holding forth on our own.

Sandra was particularly aware of not having support from the community. Her childhood had not given her much of a model for raising a family. She was the youngest and was not one to become a baby sitter as a teen. Without immediate access to relatives we were learning as we went. We survived and there were people from work and the church who were very helpful and caring. More than anything we were aware of the contrast in our families and those of our friends.

Someone has suggested that with one child you can have a "one-on-one" defense, but with twins you have to shift to "zone defense." It seemed to be true. I would come home from work and start in where I was needed. There was no clear line between my work and my wife's; it was more a battle to keep things going and stay above water. My wife had a C-section and was not able to walk easily in the weeks following their birth. I took family leave for two weeks and caught the flu. I remember a night in the first weeks when I was in the nursery holding both crying babies. I was in a delusional dream state, thinking that the ship was sinking and that I had to throw one of the children over board. Fortunately, I remember deciding that I had to keep them both. We all survived and life found a new rhythm.

But the need for money and a different lifestyle was even more apparent. A position opened at the Washington Hospital Center in the District of Columbia. It was a 900-bed hospital in the northwest of the city. The man who established the department of Pastoral Care had mismanaged some funds and had been asked to leave, so they were looking for a new Director of the Chaplain's Department. The program was under a cloud, but the position offered an exciting challenge. It also offered a significant increase in salary. We made the decision to move. It was a huge change. We left the Deep South and its culture and entered a place where there was no majority of any culture. Ronald Reagan had once visited Richmond and commented: "You know you don't have to be far from D.C. to be a long way from there." Very true. We were thrown into connection with government and military families who were used to frequent moves and making friends where they found them. We left a house in Richmond for a townhouse in Fairfax; I began to commute into the city, 45 minutes each way if traffic was moving. We began to make connections to other people who were moving into the area. The interest rates were at 18%. We moved into a new town house, and within six months the builder had gone bankrupt leaving us sitting with one other owner in a half finished building. It was 1982 and there was a change brewing in the business community. Three months after I was hired, the woman who had extended the offer to me was laid off along with 14 others in a massive restructuring of the organization. The man who now became my boss told me in our initial meeting that he was an atheist and didn't know why we even needed chaplains in the hospital. My response to him was, "Give me a little while and you'll be a Lutheran." Years later I ended up doing his father's funeral, and while I'm not sure that he became a Lutheran, he did discover something about the need for a pastor.

After getting over the shock of losing my initial boss and the anxiety of wondering if I was going to be going out in the next wave, I heard about the severance packages that the administrators received. I had never seen that much money at one time in my life and shifted from anxiety about losing my position to the side of hoping I would be laid off. But I had to stay in my job. I learned how to work in the new structure. I also opened a counseling office in Alexandria and started to develop a counseling practice as insurance against an uncertain future. I soon had others who wanted to share the office and, with that, Pastoral Counseling Associates Inc. came into being as a not-for-profit operation.

Something else happened in the process of this move and the change in my work. I had left behind a place where I had once been the student. I had gone through the paces of acquiring my tickets to function as a professional. Over time I became a peer with those who had been my teachers. It was not until I left and took on this new work that I realized that I was now a "grown up" who had the credentials to do the work I was hired to do. I realized that people looked at me as an expert in my field, I wasn't pretending to be a grown up. I was one!

The work at the hospital grew. We had started with five residents and over the first five years we added faculty and students building the department to as many as 60 students.

We added on two other hospitals and the counseling practice grew. Bob Lantz continued to be my primary advisor and mentor. We met at least monthly and he was a great source of conversation. Together we dreamed big dreams about what could happen in our work. My life at home was happy; I enjoyed my children very much. My dad did not have the permission I felt to be an active parent. I have fond memories of taking the kids to the parades for the various new presidents who came to town. To give Sandra a break on the weekends I would take all three kids down to the Mall in DC or to the shopping center. We were active in a growing congregation and I served for a couple of years as interim pastor while the church looked for new leadership. Sandra decided to enter George Mason University for a very difficult degree in French and later taught for 17 years as an English as a Second Language teacher in middle school in Fairfax County. Our children had friends that they grew up with, and while we moved to a couple of different houses, we remained in the same neighborhood, so they had a continuity that I had not had as a child and have friendships that have lasted into their adulthood.

After five years as Director of the Department of Pastoral Care, I decided to take a risk. During those five years, I had had five different bosses. For various reasons each one had either left the hospital or had taken on other work one year after another. So after the last one had been asked to leave the hospital, I decided to bid on the job. A lot of thought went into that decision. The mid-80s were a time of significant change in leadership theory. Peter Senge had emerged as a spokesperson for that changing philosophy. Paperback books outlining his theory were being published, and he himself ultimately came out with a book called *The Fifth Discipline* that outlined a systems approach to leadership including the idea of vision, shared information and trust. I was swept up in the new approach because it was much like the theory I had learned in my training in Clinical Pastoral Education. I believed that I could take that model for business leadership into the management of our group of department administrators. I approached my immediate boss and he went to his boss, the president of the hospital, and they both agreed to let me have a go at implementing the new model.

This story is a little more haphazard sounding than it actually was. My immediate boss had come to the Hospital Center a couple of years before and in our initial meeting we realized that we had met some 15 years before. He was a tall African-American man who had graduated from Georgetown University with a degree in Hospital Administration. But we first met when we were both in Memphis, Tennessee. When I was an Intern Chaplain in Memphis City Hospital he was an orderly in the Baptist Hospital next door. He and his white wife were the neighbors we had gotten to know when we were young married couples. They had moved to New Jersey when we moved to South Carolina and we had lost touch with them until that fateful day when I went to meet the newest man to head up our division. It turned out that we lived only a few blocks from each other; we both had families by then; and we were blown away by the coincidence that had brought us to that place. There is no more true statement than the one that says: "what goes around, comes around."

There was a somewhat similar connection to the president of the hospital. When he took over the hospital, he knew that he had a chaplain's department but knew little about what we did or why we were there. One day, out of the blue, he called and asked to speak to me. It seems that his wife had been recently elected warden of the vestry of their Episcopal Church and she needed someone to teach an adult Sunday school class. Was there anything I could do?

Of course when the president calls and asks for a favor, you do what you can. It was the beginning of a regular once or twice a year trip up to that church to teach a four or five week series of classes on a variety of topics. I grew close to the members of that church and was even invited to share in leading worship in a time before the Lutheran and Episcopal churches had agreed to the pulpit fellowship that we enjoy today.

So you can see it was not accidental that these two men would decide to take this risk. It was an incredible opportunity for me. For the next five years, I was the head of a table of peers who included the staff of many departments: laundry, food service, housekeeping, engineering, security, employee health, educational services, volunteers and pastoral care. I had over 3,000 employees and a huge budget responsibility. We learned to share information and work together. We built an offsite laundry, re-negotiated the food service contract, and lowered the cost for housekeeping. We worked from the theoretical base of *The Fifth Discipline* and other theory for communication and team building.

I developed a major presentation for my professional organization on the future of pastoral care in healthcare that I presented at a regional level and was then invited to present at a national level. I realized from my work in administration and in the application of our theory to practice model that the professional group that had certified me was at risk.

When the movement into clinical training had begun it was radical and experimental. It had over time moved into the main stream of hospital work. It was not unusual to find a chaplain's department and clinical training in a general or a mental hospital. The model for compensation in health care had evolved from one based on a "daily rate." Essentially that meant that the expenses of the hospital were added up each year and divided out over the number of beds in the hospital. The "daily rate" was the cost of having that bed in the system. The chaplain's department was considered part of those expenses. So when the insurance company paid the bill some of the income was for the chaplain's department.

In the early 1980's the model changed radically. The government decided to shift from the "daily rate" to the Diagnostic Related Group. This meant that a national average was developed for each hospital treatment. For instance the national rate for an appendectomy could be determined to be $100. When the hospital performed an appendectomy they would bill for $100. If it cost more than that the hospital lost money; if they could do it for less they got to keep the difference.

Two things happened here. First, with the development of effective personal computers hospitals could for the first time determine exact expenses for running various programs. Second you didn't need a chaplain to perform an appendectomy, so we shifted from being a revenue generator to becoming an expense. Health care was becoming big business, revenue was good, and expense was bad. I told my colleagues that our future was at risk. When hospitals came under pressure to reduce expenses the chaplain's department would come under close scrutiny. It was an exciting time to be in health care. I felt like I was working on the cutting edge of developing new models for leadership and pastoral care in the health care field while there were huge challenges. I completed the requirements for becoming a member of the College of Health Care Administrators even without a degree in hospital administration.

But these advances were not without their other problems. I was spending more time at work. I was losing my connection to my primary identity as a clergy. My staff and I had a great run for five years, sharing information, learning how to work together, changing the culture of the hospital's ways of accomplishing projects. But in time I had come to a crisis and had to make some soul searching decisions. My vice-president and protector had been let go, and, while he was given a good severance package, I was left unprotected, with the nursing division head gunning for me.

The head of the division did not like sharing information but rather used it as a part of her arsenal to control her staff. Over the years of my work as an Associate Administrator in the operations division she and I had clashed on numerous occasions. For instance, during a union contract negotiation I had been tasked with securing back up nurses and employees who would come in during a strike when our employees went out to the picket lines. While I was in charge of that responsibility the President and Vice-president of the hospital told me privately not to make any contracts or spend any money on those efforts. We came down to the wire and were two days away from a strike and I could not staff the hospital. The V.P. for nursing asked me for a report on where we stood and when I could not give her compete answers she upbraided me. I was alone in that room and held my own without revealing the operating instructions I was working under. Fortunately we settled at the last minute and I dodged that bullet. But there was no love lost between us.

Soon after both the president and vice-president that I had worked for were dismissed from the hospital. There was a new president of the hospital who invited me to stay with the understanding that I would take on more departments. The money was great, but I had moved a long way from my original view of vocation. Working in the hospital was like working in any other engaging workplace, you develop a work "family" and spend as much or more time with them in a given week. Even when you are not at work the challenges of work follow you home.

I began to realize that the new efficiencies of the computer and our ability to get to the actual costs of running the business reported was giving us a better sense of what was happening in the various departments of the hospital. But the efficiencies were also allowing for less direct management—creating management by the numbers. I had reached a point of responsibility that was beyond my capability to manage with integrity. The team that I had built with six departments would not be possible to maintain with a significantly increased number. I did not enjoy being buried in numbers and missed a personal connection to the work and the team. In much the same way I had arrived at a growing need for change that I experienced in my first real job at VIPCare, I was beginning to have those thoughts about taking back control over my own life. I also felt that I had learned a great deal about the management of change that I should be able to take out of the hospital to other environments.

At one point in a casual conversation with the vice-president that I reported to he began to talk wistfully about going back to school to get another degree that would allow him to teach. It sounded like a nice dream. As we talked I realized that I already had the credentials that I needed to follow that dream. Out of those thoughts the idea of creating a consulting company called Discern, Inc. emerged. I wanted to work with people and organizations in developing their full potential. That underlying theme that I had discovered in clinical training and refined in my last year of seminary continued to be an important direction for me.

So I approached the new president of the hospital with a proposal for my own severance package: six months of salary and benefits. I leased an office in Old Town Alexandria right on the river. The corporate structure that included Washington Hospital Center threw a big party during the workday and I was recognized for my ten years of work in that organization. It had been a significant time in my life. I learned a lot, was able to demonstrate the adult learning model and shared leadership concepts in that place and I left with good will and many friendships that continue until today.

Sandra had been a part of all these decisions. She felt the need for more of my attention at home. She had returned to teaching full time and her health insurance benefits covered the family in the transition. We operated in two different worlds in our professional lives. Our common connection was with the children. The local parish continued to be part of our lives and as I moved out of the hospital a part-time position opened in that congregation. I was able to develop a program for adult education with a class that grew to some

80 people on a Sunday morning. I participated in regular worship and in the preaching schedule. Our children were active in the swim team and I ended up as president of the pool board, working to keep that operation solvent and alive. While I was busy developing my practice and the work at the church I was based in the community and was more available for the family.

The transition was not as hard as I might have expected. I did not miss the long commute into the city. I liked my new office and the idea of working on my own. I enrolled in a training program in the work *The Fifth Discipline* did and paid my own expenses to attend a week's workshop in Boston. The idea of developing a sense of vision for an organization along with the focus on the team were important components of the training model. Another of the disciplines was a model for creating ideas and making them a reality. Senge had used the work of another man, Robert Fritz, who had written of his experience as an artist and musician. From his own work he developed a model for looking at how a creative idea is surfaced and worked through to a completed project or piece of music or art. There was additional training in that work and I followed my curiosity to his seminars and training.

I hoped to bring my experience and this training to the work place, to work with leaders and their teams in developing a working model for the new workforce. As I had already seen, the computer was beginning to bring major change to the work place and even now we are working on models for work in this century. My original vision was one of working with corporate leadership in developing new models for interaction. That vision was not lived out in the ways I would have expected, but in the process I learned even more about the idea of vocation and ways to work with people in finding meaning in their lives. Leaving the hospital culture allowed me to look at various options and over time I found my work and home life working together.

Sandra had followed a traditional path of working as a schoolteacher and sharing the schedule for class and vacation with our children. She worked at school and in the evening spent much time grading papers and preparing for the next day. We did evolve a relationship that allowed us to share the work of managing our home and family even before the concept of "Leaning In" had become popular. It was interesting that the work that Sandra did with the kids was expected and the time that I spent with them was looked on as exceptional.

We grew up in a time of change in the expectations of the roles and men and women that continue to the present time. I had a lot to learn.

One of the companies I connected with was a health insurance practice that was owned and directed by a very energetic and creative man. He understood health insurance and he worked out the first models for health savings accounts as an insurance model. He ultimately was involved with Congress in setting up the legal model for what has become a regular part of the health insurance industry. I worked closely with him and went on to be licensed to sell health insurance. We were not ultimately successful, but I enjoyed the relationship with the staff and the excitement of presenting a new idea in the work world. His concept was simple: you took out high-end insurance, the best money could buy, with a very high deductible. Then you created a medical savings account that you built up to include the full amount of the deductible. It put the individual in charge of their own health care; they could choose who they wanted to see and what treatment they wanted. They were paying for it directly so the idea was that they would be more astute shoppers for health care services and if they faced a difficult diagnosis they would be covered by the most comprehensive insurance available. In the end this particular venture did not succeed and I did not make any money on my investment of time and effort. But I had no regrets and later when I took over the leadership of an organization with need for an employee health insurance plan we called on this company for their services.

In the midst of setting up my own company I went to visit one of my former bosses. He had been given a liberal severance plan that included an office and full secretarial services. We talked for a while and I met the principles in the out-placement company that had his contract. Ultimately, I became a major contractor with them. I worked with executives like my former boss. I would be given a group of people who had been given their final packages in their current work and would now have to seek other employment. I was also assigned executives who had been given severance packages that included long-term consultation as they looked for their next employer. I learned how to teach under stress, because each class filled out evaluations of the instructor and your next assignment depended on how well you had done the session before. I enjoyed the work and the relationships. I developed a series of lectures that I used in the consulting work and at the church.

From those lectures came my first book, *Get a Life: A Second Chance After Fifty*. I saw the book as a necessary step in building my business. I needed a "leave behind" that

I could use both in my work and in securing work in the future. Over time I became one of the lead professionals in Right Associates and had developed a specialty in working with clients who wanted to go out in their own. I submitted a proposal to the company that we establish a specific division in the office that identified those more entrepreneurial persons so that we might work with them early on to use their benefit packages to support their start-up operation. The local office liked my idea, but the national organization was not convinced so the idea was not implemented. One of the interesting things about living and working in Washington, DC was the sense that our area was about five years ahead of the rest of the country in innovation. What we were attempting in our area would not filter out to other areas for years.

What I started out to do with Discern, Inc. as a consulting company for business leadership was only partially realized. I was enjoying the work with Right Associates, with the health insurance company and with the local church. Somehow we were making ends meet and I had achieved my goal of retuning home and being more a part of the family. My kids were growing up and I was enjoying watching them as they participated in the school and swim team and were preparing to go off to college. Our church had developed an extensive drama program, putting on a major musical and dinner theater each year. We would convert the sanctuary into a theater and members of the church would play various roles in the drama. My daughters and I participated in these presentations and we enjoyed the many hours of rehearsal and down time around those musicals.

In the middle of this work and life I began to develop the idea for a cross-country bicycle trip.

Webster's New World Dictionary defines the adjective "epic" as "like an epic; heroic; grand." So I guess that an Epic Journey could be considered a heroic or grand trip or adventure. To me it has been much more than that and at the same time not something I have considered either heroic or even grand.

I was approaching the twenty-fifth anniversary of my ordination. I felt like it was an appropriate time to acknowledge that milestone. I had recently come through some major events in both my personal and professional life that I needed to reflect on. So I put out the word of my interest in riding a bike across the United States during the year of 1995 and a good friend took up the challenge, thinking that his sons would also join our adventure. As it turned out, they decided against the trip, but a senior in college who had just graduated and whose job would not start until the fall asked to join us. That was the beginning of the first ride.

Interestingly there is some precedent for this idea from early times. The Israelites are finally lead out of Egypt into the desert and find that they have to wander for 40 years (or a long time) before they are able to make their claim on the promised land. In the New Testament Jesus comes to John for baptism and immediately, according to Matthew, Mark and Luke, goes from standing in the river to spending 40 days in the desert by himself without food and water while he resists the temptations to power and status. The record of that experience would have to have come from Jesus; there were no disciples there to witness his own experience of that time. He returns and begins three years of travel and teaching, knowing all the while that he is headed to Jerusalem and to ultimate death.

I certainly don't put myself in a circle with Moses or Jesus, but there are many other accounts of epic journey that suggest that this need for a time apart is not unique. Bill Bryson's *A Walk in the Woods*, Stephen E. Ambrose's *Undaunted Courage*, and Cheryl Strayed's *Wild* are just a few of the books I've read over the years that tell stories of risk and discovery that are both factual accounts of new lands discovered and at the same time new understanding of self found as a result of the epic trip.

Celebrating 25 years of ministry then now seems a bit premature compared to my current 45-year tenure, but at the time it seemed like a good thing to do.

It was time to take a trip!

The three of us packed up our gear and our bicycles and flew from the Baltimore Airport to San Diego. We reassembled our bikes and rode out of the airport and started the trip home. The initial weeks were very difficult; it is hard to train for a ride like this, so those first two weeks became the training ground. We climbed out of the city up into the mountains in the summer heat, camping the first night in the backyard of a fire station. The firemen were concerned for our safety in an area where illegal immigration was a problem. We rode through the desert at night and slept during the day to avoid the intense heat. Over time, we developed a pattern. We would look at the maps and determine our next stop. We ate in all-you-can-eat restaurants, and when we couldn't camp we found cheap hotels to share. We rode six days a week and rested on the seventh. I went to the Catholic Church for Mass every Saturday night. I carried the book The Artist's Way and used that process to reflect on my past experience. I began a regular practice of journaling that I have continued since that time. I was into a type of Eastern stretching program that I practiced every day, a precursor to my current yoga practice. We met a number of interesting and helpful people. I began to be interested in the connection between diet and energy. We grew stronger and in the end finished the trip in five weeks, a week earlier than expected. We had ridden 3,000 miles and averaged 100 miles a day for that time. I lost 15 pounds and was in peak physical shape at the end of the trip.

It was out of that trip that my sense of direction became clearer and the book that I wrote grew out of that time and effort. It was one of those events in my life that has defined me and gave meaning to my life. Often people would say something about wishing that they could do something like what we were doing and I would invite them to join us. It begins with getting on the bike.

My first epic journey was a celebration of a quarter of a century working in a profession. The fact that it was ordained ministry added a different dimension. Even before ordination I had been introduced to a specialized method of ministry that challenged and excited me. I had pursued the training and credentials that I needed to work in the field of education for clergy and in providing pastoral counseling. I had successfully worked in congregations as pastor and educator and maintained a close connection to that part of ministry as well. As I have mentioned, the underlying theory of the educational model I was caught up in was developed by John Dewey and was called Experiential Education. Following this model meant that one learned from experience and the pursuit of the next level of interest determined the education, theory, and learning that would be needed. The students and the clients that I worked with learned from me and I learned from them. I often felt that I was only a short distance ahead of them—if that—and even today often feel that I teach myself just before I pass that knowledge on to others.

One theory suggests that we have three choices in the way we will face anxiety. We can bind it. In other words we can deny that it exists and live as though it didn't. When you begin to bind any feeling, all the other feelings are drawn in and you end up with the inability to feel. There is only the response of the intellect, not of empathy or of expectation. Life becomes black or white with no subtlety, no grace for one's self or another.

A second choice is the most popular, avoidance. We look at a difficult situation, a hard decision, the need to change a habit whatever it is that causes our anxiety and we put it off, deny it, and avoid it. Finally when push comes to shove, we make a decision, we act and often discover that the worry about it was more trouble than the actual experience of going through whatever was causing us concern.

The final approach is one of anxiety approaching. That happens when one sees a difficult issue and moves toward it rather than denying it existence or attempting to avoid it. The more experience a person has with approaching anxiety the more natural it becomes. Many people who have expressed the wish that they could take a bike ride across the U.S. will almost immediately counter that wish with some reality statement about their physical ability or their circumstances that would make a trip like that impossible. I know by now that either the person is just making conversation and has no real interest in a ride like that, which is not unusual, or they don't want to think about what a trip like that could mean to them and what keeps them from it. That's an extreme example, but life is full of choices.

After returning from the bike ride across the country, I settled into my practice, working with the international out-placement company taking individuals and groups through career development exercises and process. I continued to have a counseling practice and I was working on the staff of a local Lutheran church that was our family's congregation. I developed an adult education program and was available for other pastoral duties.

Along with swim team and church activities, we took summer vacations to be with Sandra's family and to spend time at the beach or in the mountains of North Carolina. We were connected to the community around us and life was good.

In the middle of all of that was going on I got a call from my Bishop. Sounds simple enough—people call all the time—but for me there is a difference between a call and a Call, and this was a Call. The Lutheran Social Service of the National Capital Area was two weeks away from bankruptcy; their executive director had been relieved of his position. Initially, it was to be a consulting project: "fix it or close it" was the Bishop's request. I assumed when the Bishop called that he was hopeful that we could pull it out, but I learned several years later that he would have preferred that it close. I'm not sure that even he knew that at the time.

In the Lutheran tradition, you can graduate from seminary, but you cannot be ordained until you have a call. If you should leave your call and go on a status of "awaiting a call," you could be in that status for three years. After that you returned to the higher calling, gave up ordination and became a part of the priesthood of all believers. I had been operating under a call to the local parish and now would move to a call for specialized ministry for the synod of the church.

I mentioned in the first chapter of this work that at one point my dad was operating under a "call" when he left a parish in Austin, Texas for one in Baton Rouge, Louisiana. At that point in my life I considered that a sacred act. He was operating out of a commitment to something outside himself. I assumed that he had attempted to hear God's will in that invitation and having heard that will he acted on what he believed to be his call.

I have operated with the same belief system. When I have been approached by an opportunity, I assume that there is something else operating in addition to my self-interest. But how to sort that out is not always easy. Looking back at that point into my career I can say that something beyond me was at work. I ended up at seminary because I didn't know what else to do. I didn't have a model for working in business or as a lawyer. I had a degree in economics and four years of experience as a politician, but my dad's model was my primary template for career direction. Ending up in a parish after my first year without a supervising pastor and being offered an opportunity for an introduction to Clinical Pastoral Education both as a model for learning and as a direction for my career formed a powerful turning point in my life. I followed the call to the parish in Miami and persisted in leaving for training rather than staying where I was wanted and was comfortable. Even at that time a psychologist friend suggested that I go to the V.A. hospital system for training. In the early 70s, there were positions for education and a PhD being offered in those training settings. I consciously choose not to follow that invitation. I was very clear about wanting to maintain my pastoral identity. There is a very real tension here between what I "want" and what I am "being lead toward." It's called "free-will" in theological circles. But discerning one's own selfish will from God's is tricky to say the least. Ultimately I believe that God can work with whatever I decide. It is only after that fact that one can look back and see from the eyes of faith that something more was operating in a decision-making process than was obvious at the time. I answered the call.

Wading into Lutheran Social Services was a challenge. Morale was down and the banks were calling with questions about our ability to meet our mortgage payment. There was also the problem of the every two-week payroll. I quickly discovered that we did not have a problem of income; we had a problem of collections and accounts receivable. We started pounding on the D.C. governmental agencies with which we had major contracts for payments that we were owed. I took the executive committee of our board to meet with the bank's vice president. She was as cold as ice and beyond being cynical. The bank had not been kept informed about what had been happening and to say that they weren't happy would not come close to the truth. She really didn't want to own a part of Georgia Avenue where the property was located in one of the rougher parts of Washington, but she didn't cut us any slack. We persuaded her somehow that we just needed some time. As we began to recover, we sought out a new bank and by Christmas I was pleased to open new accounts and end our relationship with that bank and banker.

I worked to build a leadership team and with the three groups within the agency, Adoption/Foster Care, Immigration Services, and Mental Health Services, to stabilize their operations and bring their contracts into line with expectations. Our team worked through a process called Scenario Planning that had been developed by British Petroleum. Using their template, we developed plans for worst case, best case and something-in-between scenarios. We developed outlines for action in either situation and went to the board with our analysis of where we were and our hopes for a meaningful future. The Board was relieved and energized and endorsed the plan with one condition: that I would give up my contractual status and join the organization as the Executive Director.

I accepted the invitation and left the consulting practice and my own company. The need for my book slipped away. I now look back and see that there were threads running throughout. When I took the first bike ride I used it to raise money for Lutheran Social Services, and I delivered a check for $8,000 dollars at the end of the ride. I had a long-term interest in the social ministries of the church. Lutherans are good at this stuff. The underlying theme of Abraham welcoming the strangers that came to his tent and in that welcome discovering an opportunity to serve God was a theme of our agency and very much resonated with me.

Through all this change I continued to find time to ride my bike on the weekends, join the annual Bike Virginia ride wherever it went, and to start to dream about another long ride. The company whose maps we had used to ride from San Diego back to Virginia was originally called Bike Centennial; they developed the maps for the many groups that rode across America to celebrate that the country's birthday. They had changed their name to Adventure Cycling and I had joined as member of their organization. With membership comes a regular journal that details trips made by various people on bikes and updates of the latest maps that were available. A new route had been researched and mapped. It had taken ten years to develop and was first attempted in 1998, but of the 13 people who attempted the trip, only ten finished it 72 days later. I ordered a set of maps and read the introduction.

The first of six maps listed a number of cautions: "hot and dry weather, water filter mandatory . . .. We discourage you from attempting to ride the route solo . . .. Minimum group of three, so that one can stay with an injured person while the other goes for help . . .. You'll encounter a lot of incredible things as you pedal this route: wildlife, historic mining districts, beautiful wetlands and not-so-beautiful clear cuts, and much more. One thing you won't see a lot of, however, is motorized traffic."

I was hooked. In addition to putting maps together, Adventure Cycles puts together groups for a fee. The group I was looking at would be the third group they would take on the trip. We would have two guides, both guys who could repair bikes and knew how to teach us to prepare food for a group of ten or more. We would not be "supported" by a trailing vehicle, i.e., we would carry everything we needed on our bikes. We would even carry our food and water as needed; often we would leave one town and would not see another for several days. We would take turns cooking. We would sleep in tents. Most of us would decide to pull a one-wheel trailer instead of saddlebags to carry our gear. The trails would be dirt roads, fire paths, and single tracks most of the time in wilderness areas of the country. It is the longest mountain bike trail in the world: 2,465 miles crossing back and forth across the Continental Divide over 30 times.

This was not a spontaneous decision. I thought a lot about the trip, my family, and my work. There is never a good time to take a ride like this except perhaps when one has retired and there is more time. But at that time in my life, I don't think that I expected to live to retirement. Both of my grandfathers had died of heart attacks when they were 63, and my dad had emergency by-pass surgery when he was 63. Because I was conscious of taking better care of myself, I thought that I would make it to the magical age of 63, but who knew how long after that.

My children were at good ages for me to be away for a three-month stint. My oldest daughter would be 24 and the twins were 19. The oldest was graduating and the twins were leaving for college. It was perhaps the feeling of seeing them grow up and leave home that was also contributing to my need for another trip. They were leaving home in search of a new identity apart from the family, just as I was looking for what my identity would be for the future. Finally, there was within me a need to prove myself as a man, as one who could face a difficult task and survive. I did not go to Viet Nam; I hadn't passed the endurance test of military service. I had faced challenges of various sorts including the bike ride across the country. But I still questioned my ability to survive under tough circumstances. I wrote in my journal on the first day of the trip:

> *"I find myself on the edge of sadness, loss of family and friends. I feel small and unsure of myself at various points. Am I up to this trip? Is it more than I can handle? Do I have too much equipment, the right equipment? Will I be able to stand the test? Beyond that is the question of what will come of*

this trip. Will I study yoga? Will I find a new sense of my own faith – what am I here for and what would it mean for me to move toward the light?"

I had the dream stirring inside for two years. Ever since hearing about the trip I had been moving in that direction. Sandra was never against my trips. In fact, we had started out with our first adult bikes in Miami—actually, it was her very first bike, a three-speed Schwinn. We started with matching bikes, but I traded up to a ten-speed within six months. We grew to enjoy walking and hiking together and she was able to take her own trips to Europe and South America together and on her own and with our daughters. This trip was a little daunting to consider, but I don't remember any real resistance on her part and for that I am thankful. The kids cheered me on. My oldest daughter had come home in the first semester of her junior year in college saying that she needed to take time off from school and wanted to take her pick-up truck (her choice of vehicle) and travel around the U.S. with a girlfriend. I supported her, her mother less so, but she went and it turned out to be a trip to discover our extended family and to find herself. She had a real adventure and went back to college the next fall and graduated with her class. Over the years my twins have also risked taking trips that were out of the ordinary and I have to think that my trips provided them an example and at least took away any hesitancy that I might have otherwise registered.

The decision had basically been made. So that only left the job. I approached the board with a request to have a sabbatical for three months. Again, there was no resistance. We had a good team in place, and I planned to check in every week with the office. They gave me their blessing. I had a great board chair that was supportive and persuasive and I am sure that his support was crucial. Besides, the board included a number of men and women my age that had dreams of their own and wanted to see someone live one out.

So, having run out of excuses, the door was open. I tried to start training, but as with the earlier trip I found that it was hard to duplicate the experience of riding between 50 and 60 miles a day while pulling all your goods in the world behind you for a week at a time. I went to the local bike shop and asked their advice in buying a mountain bike, but it turned out that they didn't have a grasp of what the trip would entail and the bike that they recommended at $700 was about $1,000 short of what the others would bring to the trip. The tent I bought lasted about two weeks before I shipped home the broken fiberglass poles and replaced it with a tent with aluminum poles that was designed for major weather. This was the first of many lessons: spend the money! Don't try to get by on the cheap, because it never pays. I ended up replacing the back wheel of the bike with a burley wheel that carried me the rest of the way, but not before several breakdowns of original equipment.

I said goodbye to staff, church and family and flew off to Whitefish, Montana to begin day one of a 75-day bike trip of a lifetime. Thirteen other people had signed on and we would have two guides. After a brief orientation, we left by truck for the Canadian border and from there began our trip. The first week was a shake down. We were riding back to Whitefish, learning how to camp, put up bear bags, and cook for one another. We discovered our styles as riders: some of us got up early and were off, while others would sleep in and arrive in camp much later. Twelve members of the group were men and the two guides were men, which left Sue, the one woman. Our ages varied from the mid-20s for a couple of the guys, to the oldest, a Frenchman named Pierre who was 70 and had only limited English skills. I was 57; there were two men in their mid-60s. Early on I settled in with a Brit, named Pat, who was in his late 30s. We started out the first day and would continue that pattern until he suffered a back injury and had to drop out for a time. Sue and Pierre joined us and the four of us took care of each other as the trip unfolded and we settled into our routines. By the end of the first week, three of the men had decided to withdraw. I noted in my journal that I had an open ticket to fly home and could have gotten on the plane but never considered that option.

Camping in the wilderness of Montana is unforgettable. The stars at night are unbelievable. The trails were rough and even in that early June period there was snow on the ground in some places. We would occasionally come to ice-fed streams that we had to portage across, which meant taking off shoes and socks and wading into the stream to push the bike and then the trailer to the other side, putting our socks and shoes back on frozen feet, and then peddling off down the road. We all had big bells on our bikes and we carried bear spray in the event that we came up unexpectedly on a bear, especially a mother bear and her cubs. Our talking and ringing bells were hopefully enough warning and, while we did spot some bears that first week, we were at a safe distance. The idea was that when the bear was charging you head on, you were supposed to hold your ground until you could see the whites of their eyes then spray them with the pepper spray and hope that you weren't facing into a head wind. This strategy somehow did not give me much confidence. I was glad that I didn't have to test it out.

We would ride from early morning with occasional stops and snacks. We prepared sandwiches before we left each day for lunch. At night we would sit with each other and study the maps, trying to determine how far to try for the next day and where we would plan to camp. If there was a town en route, we would use those visits to buy food for the next days; if the timing was right, we would camp nearby.

As I mentioned, in those first weeks, I had bike repairs that I needed and for the most part our guides were able to make do until we could get to a place with parts that we might need. One of my worst days on the trip was when in the midst of a cold blowing rain, my rear tire went out of true and the unbalanced wheel caused the rim to heat up, so the back tire blew out. In the cold mud, I was taking the trailer loose and getting out the new tire. A couple of people stopped to help including Sue. When I pulled out a patched tube she said loudly and pointedly, "You are using patched tubes." I could have melted into the mud and I have never used a patched tube since, and our friendship survived her sarcasm. The tire was remounted, and I rode without the rear breaks until we got to camp and could true the wheel.

We would ride for a week or so at a time and then take a long weekend break. Those were good times. I cleaned up my bike and got my gear back in shape. I had a regular routine on the trip of journaling when I first woke and I intended to read deeply while on the trip and I did. When I finished a book, I would ship it home and start on the new one. I read about yoga and its practice and philosophy. I had just begun to practice yoga when I left for the trip. I also read about Indian culture, philosophy, theology and religious studies. I would use the time riding to reflect on my reading and I enjoyed the opportunity for long periods of deep thought. When you are pulling everything you own, any extra weight is to be avoided, but the books were important to me and worth the effort.

Montana was my favorite territory of the trip: the woods, the clear air, the lakes and rivers with their ice-cold waters were amazing. The maps for the route proved to be as good as the ones I had used before. If you got to a place where you felt a turn was needed that was not on the map, you soon discovered that the map was right. The roads were dirt for the most part, often washboard in effect. There were many times when the climbs were so steep that I had to get off and push the bike--no shame there, we all did it. Having a trailer on the back meant you were pulling it up the hill as well and when you came down the other side, it was pushing you.

Colorado was also a beautiful state, with lush valleys and scenes of hot air balloons floating past. As we came into New Mexico in August, there was shortage of water. Often we would come to places that were noted as having water, a stream or whatever, only to find a dry river bed. We pumped water through our filters that we would never have considered before. At one point of the trip we had divided into two groups because some of our members had developed giardia, an intestinal disorder that left you dehydrated. I was shepherding our group along and one of the guides, a man in his 20s who had proven to be fairly narcissistic, and I went up a dry riverbed in search of water. We finally found some suspicious puddles and began to filter the water. After a time he put his water bottle aside and said, "Well, I have my water." I almost came off the ground to attack him, but let him know that we were getting water for our group, not just ourselves. It was one of the few times on the trip I felt that much anger.

The other major emotional experience of the trip for me began when I was talking to Sandra at a phone outside a bar in the middle of nowhere and she told me that her mother had a re-occurring cancer and would have to be treated. I knew at that moment that her mother would not survive and I was devastated. After I hung up, I biked back to our camp, tears flowing, and began writing her a long letter of appreciation for all that she had done for me and for our family. My handwriting is not stellar, and I understand that, after she got the letter, she and the daughter who was taking care of her would spend time in the afternoon trying to figure out what I had written. But even with those difficulties she appreciated what I was able to say to her. During the last week of the trip, word came that my mother-in-law was in the hospital in the last stages of life. I tried to see if there was a way home, but there wasn't, so I spent the time of her funeral writing about the meaning of this trip and of her life and its gift. I needed to finish the trip, but I regretted not being there with my family in that time of loss. My mother-in-law had spent most of her life in a little town in North Carolina, rarely traveling often or far. She extended herself to us in her cooking, sewing and affection, and I think she marveled at our lives and the places we had been and who we had become. I am sure she thought I was a little crazy and she had never known a preacher like me, but in spite of it all, I felt her love with much appreciation.

As the trip came to an end, the group had enough money in our food budget to have one last major dinner together. Pat the Brit had rejoined our group and we had ridden hard to the end. At the banquet he took charge and went around the table giving us awards that he had made up. When he came to me, he described me as a leader and as having strength and courage. I was deeply touched by his recognition. I had acknowledged to myself some sense of my leadership skills before this trip, mainly that I did not mind taking on responsibility and I enjoyed working with people to accomplish a task. But I did not have a great sense of myself as being strong or brave.

In this journey, I had discovered something about myself: that I could take care of others and myself. I could push on through difficulties and make accommodations as needed. Over the course of the trip I had reached deep within my feelings to understand my love for my family and my mother-in-law, and I learned things about being alone and surviving that sustains me even today. Finally, I took on a new sense of identity. I had known myself as a pastor, teacher, husband, father, but I now knew of myself as an adventurer. When I got on that Schwinn Blue Hornet and rode out of the parsonage some years earlier, I had no idea where that bike would take me. The bike as a means of transportation still fits me well, and I have other dreams and trips yet to ride.

I returned to my work at LSS. I had been there for three years and I would remain for seven more. We put together a good team with my CFO and HR director; we had four divisions and good people who had had long careers in their fields. A very creative man who had raised money for other organizations joined us. He came to us as a consultant. He became a good friend. The woman I had used as a publicist for my book became our marketing person. So we had a complete team and we began to develop a vision about what we might become. We looked at ways to become less dependent on government contracts: we tried to develop real estate that would generate revenue and help us with the gentrification that DC was beginning to experience. We would get close to success only to be pushed back at the last hurdle. Because we had the title "Lutheran" in our name there was an expectation that we should be able to raise money from the Lutheran community in our area. That was a good idea except for the other ten agencies in the region that were approaching the same donors. The National Lutheran Home was taking the biggest slice of the pie as good Lutherans came to their facility in their last days. The rest of us did fund raisers, walks, and marketing with good stories about our clients and their needs. But these efforts would never make up for the decreasing money from the city contracts mixed with increased expectations for services. I realize now that another issue was the decreasing membership in the church.

The church that I attended had not experienced the loss that other congregations faced. We had an excellent senior pastor, a good music and youth program, a drama program and a preschool with an excellent reputation. Lord of Life was not losing members, but it was not growing either. In my later work I would come to the realization that the Lutheran brand was no longer a draw as I watched the church in the Virginia Synod grow smaller each year.

Near the end of my term at LSS I made one last effort to create a new vision for the future. I engaged a consultant that I had met on other occasions and we traveled to NYC for a day of reflection with two other experts in the field. In the morning I laid out where our agency found itself and by lunchtime we were all depressed and without hope. We went to lunch and came back to a revelation. What if we took the organization completely out of the contract service effort, sold our properties, cut back on our administrative staff and became a consulting organization that could assist congregations in the synod in developing their own dreams and social ministries that would be appropriate to their communities. It was brilliant. We would be able to have a small endowment from the property sale and we could be a resource to congregations that were struggling.

I came back with excitement and prepared to present to the board. Initially they got caught up in the excitement, but then they realized that to make that decision would mean no longer being a provider of adoption and foster care services. They could not take that step. The problem was that we were in an all or nothing position. Either we gave up the buildings and the infrastructure like the HR person and the CFO, and took our chance as a resource to the church or we had to maintain the structure in order to have the contract that gave us entree to the adoption and foster care, mental health, and immigration contracts. You could not secure those contracts if you could not demonstrate that infrastructure. So we decided to end the mental health contract. It was our largest and most difficult contract. The leadership in the city was not reliable and the provision of services was becoming increasingly difficult while the revenue was decreasing. It was a hard decision and some of the most painful work of my career. I had to lay off 35 of our staff and move our clients to other agencies. The Mental Health leadership in the city did not help and in fact attacked me personally. My board chair, a retired city contractor, thought that he could do my job better than I could and was not supportive. We survived; the agency survived and is there today. I decided to leave and the board chair took over. Within six months he and the new director he hired were gone as well. The woman who took over after that had been on our staff before in development and she has done a great job of keeping the agency alive and functioning.

In the midst of all this change another door began to open. One of the faculty at the Medical College of Virginia Department of Patient Counseling had retired and they needed a CPE Supervisor. My mentor Bob Lantz and others encouraged me to consider the move. Much like an earlier time in my career when I said that I would "never go back to Miami," I had similar feelings about a return to Richmond. But I was tired and knew that I needed a change.

The interview went well in Richmond and the city seemed to have changed. There was a more open feeling in the community and we would be able to live in the inner city with no concern for the schools for our kids. It was a much different time for me and I decided to make the move. Sandra was ready to retire from middle school teaching and, while it took us six months to make the move, we were able to find a home and settle into the new community.

My expectation was that as faculty that I would be able to develop my writing skills and would not have to deal with administrative duties to any great degree. It was short-lived expectation. In the month I took off after leaving LSS before I began at MCV I wrote a paper called "Losing," a lengthy paper on my experience with ten years in social ministry. I had just read Jack Welch's book *Winning* about his stellar career at GE and the money he had made. I was on the other side of the table.

I moved to Richmond, joined a writing group, and began to get back into the supervision and teaching of students, upgrading my credentials when the Chair of the department decided to move up into the Dean's office on a full time basis. It was a good move for him and not surprising: he was an able administrator and had been a great chair for our department. But his leaving created a dilemma: should I apply for the chair position or take my chances on who the next chair would be and whether or not I would be content with that leadership. I had not stepped up earlier in my career when the leader at VIPCare stepped down and I had ended up working for someone that was not the best choice. So I applied and went through the interview. Bob Lantz was very much in the background, having been a continuing supporter of the department over many years and someone held in high regard by the Dean. The interview went well. I understood that there was an expectation that the department needed to develop other markets for students outside the hospital. The university expected growth in numbers and our department had grown as large as it could within the hospital. I took on the challenge and began to develop a connection within the community for a parish based training program. We hired another supervisor on a contractual basis to work in that program. She had excellent experience in long distance training and we began to develop a creative program of training using the newest technology for long-distance teaching. At the same time the department as a whole had not bought into the expectation of growth outside the hospital and were resistant to the change. I did not do a good job of developing the vision in a way that included them.

In the midst of that growth and change two things occurred. The university got a new president who was more focused on academics and research than growth and Bob Lantz became ill with a rare form of cancer and died rather suddenly.

I had maintained my relationship with Bob for 40 plus years and his death was a great loss for me. I visited with him in that last week of his life and participated in his funeral.

We discovered that Bob's will was outlined but not final and over the next couple of years I worked with his wife and niece to settle his estate in a way that would honor his wishes. As a result the department now has an endowed Chair position in his name and another endowed position, a faculty position, in his wife's name. There will always be some sort of CPE training position at the Medical College of Virginia. Katherine Lantz also established a foundation that would seek to provide educational opportunities for clergy in the Northern Neck of Virginia and I have enjoyed maintaining our relationship over the years since Bob's death.

About the same time that Bob died my mother came to the end of her life. She lived in Texas after my dad's death but after a time decided to move back to Brevard, North Carolina to be close to my second youngest brother. He and his wife were moving there to be close to their daughter and ultimately to retire there. There was a very nice continuing care facility that would provide mother an apartment that she could afford. She sold her lake house and made the move. It was good to have her closer by and I knew that I needed to make an effort to finish any outstanding issues with her. We visited with her a couple of time a year and I tried to talk with her at a meaningful level, but it was not to be. She gloried in all that my brothers and I accomplished and she would bore others endlessly with stories about our successes. She told each of us about what our brothers and their families had done, but she never shared her praise with us directly.

At one point while I was still in DC I was invited to offer a prayer at the opening of the House of Representatives. A friend had set it up for me, an honor. I invited her to go with me. We met my friend, and joined the Chaplain of the House for lunch in the Congressional dining room and she was there when I offered the prayer I had written. Later I gave her a copy of the Congressional Record that included the prayer. I think she was pleased. She certainly shared the news with my brothers. She had three sons who were ordained Lutheran clergy; none of us was interested in becoming a Bishop, to her great disappointment.

One experience that I had in the last years of her life was a time when I laughed as hard as I've ever laughed. Mother was in the hospital when were down in the area for a visit. As I mentioned at an earlier time, Mother wasn't much of a cook, but whatever she had was always available for visitors. Our family took in orphans and visitors over the years. After I had left home, a man came to Baton Rogue who needed a place to stay. He was from Iran, young and alone. He moved into my parent's home and lived there for some months while he attended LSU. Just as mysteriously as he had arrived he left and mother never heard from him.

While mother was in the hospital she happened to watch the international news when the new Prime Minister of Iran was introduced, Mahmoud Ahmadinejad. My mother took one look at the newscast and was convinced that Mahmoud was the same man who had lived with her. They did look somewhat alike. I started laughing so hard that staff from the hospital came to her room to see if there was a concern.

This was my mom's chance: she didn't get a Bishop, but she could have a President of Iran. I thought that maybe she could broker world peace or, from a darker side, maybe his anger at the USA was a result of his extended stay at my mother's.

Mother didn't get along with her daughters-in-law—an understatement. There were times when she would call our home and if Sandra answered the phone mother would ask to speak to her son, Dr. Mark Cooper. But it was not Sandra alone; all the daughters-in-law wished her well but were not able to make peace with her. When she was on her college trip around the country my oldest daughter stopped for a month at my mother's. Mother welcomed her and her friend in and they had a good time resting, working for a time at McDonald's and seemed to enjoy her by handing her insults right back to her. Maybe Jennifer found the secret.

In the end she began to get old and knew she was near death. She called us all home and we went. We had a nice weekend together, no major break through; she just wanted us all there. Two weeks later we went back for her funeral. I had given up on being angry with her, tried to protect my wife from her, and spent some time with her.

Erikson says that we need to forgive our parents for not being the parents we needed and that our parents need to forgive their children for not being the children they would have wanted. I think that we arrived at that place.

I have also heard it said that if you don't have the family you wanted, find one that you do want. I found that family with Sandra's parents. Her mother didn't know what to make of me, with my work and my crazy trips, but she was a caring soul to me and to our children. She was an amazing cook. She suffered a lot of pain in her life but she still had a smile for us and loved my kids deeply. I still regret missing being with her at the end and was glad that she was able to spend time reading my letter and knew how much I appreciated and loved her.

Sandra's dad had also been important to me. I had my dad on a high pedestal, but Mr. Greene was just a guy and I enjoyed hanging out with him. We cut grass, worked in the yard, and enjoyed a good story and a steak dinner. He had been mean and abusive to his children and there were still some hints of that behavior, but he never went there with me and he was careful around our children. I know that he was proud of his daughter and all that she accomplished. He thought that we had crossed over to the other side of the tracks, but I respected him and we maintained our relationship. He could be funny, was self-educated and one hell of a salesman. I enjoyed making some of those sales trips with him and watching him befriend his customers in the laundry and dry cleaning business, reminiscent of my Granddaddy Billy.

After six years of work in the Department of Patient Counseling I took a full summer off to be with family. Sandra had been diagnosed with a chronic illness and I wanted to have more time for her and family.

Sandra's illness began simply enough: she had gone to give blood and had been told that her blood count was too low, that she should go home, and have the count checked out. So she went for additional testing. It was the beginning of a diagnostic process that would determine her condition: a non-cancerous blood problem called Myclodysplasia Syndrome (MDS) or "bone marrow failure disorder." Put simply, her body had stopped producing enough red blood cells. We, like everyone else who has a major diagnosis, went to the Internet to find what we could. The stories there were all the same: the disease was progressive, and as time went on, blood transfusions would be necessary to continue to live. Then the stories would trail off.

During that time off the Rector of the church we had been attending since our move to Richmond approached me with a job offer. St James' is a unique downtown church in Richmond that has a long and deep history in Richmond. During the months before we moved I had attended Lutheran churches in the community and did not feel welcomed in any of them.

We were unpacking our kitchen in our new home after our move to Richmond. I had seen this old church in our neighborhood and persuaded Sandra that we should visit, I told her that it was an inner city church that was probably dying and that their 9 o'clock service was probably a Matins that we could be in and out in 45 minutes! Besides who wanted to unpack the kitchen? Well, when we got there we discovered a beautiful sanctuary that had been rebuilt after a major fire some years back. It was Confirmation Sunday, the church was packed, all 450 seats filled. The choir was amazing, and there were 50 kids being confirmed. It was amazing.

The Rector, Randy Hollerith, had welcomed us into that community from the beginning of our first visit. In the weeks that followed the pastor invited me to lunch and the rest is history. I became a consultant to the church and later joined the choir. We volunteered in various ministries. I was invited to teach in the Adult Forum and later to preach and share in celebrating the Sacrament. I let my Bishop know where I would be attending church and in those days of pulpit fellowship he seemed to have no concern. I have had the benefit over my adult life of being connected to active, creative congregations, in Miami, in Richmond the first time, in Northern Virginia and now back in Richmond.

At this point some six years after we had moved into the community Randy asked if I would consider joining his staff. Their retired clergy who handled visitation was retiring again and Randy wanted to split the position between me and another retired clergy in the congregation. I was ready to close one door when this new door opened. I left my work at the hospital and joined the staff at St. James'. I was able to be more available at home and could continue to be involved in visitation, teaching and celebration. Over the four years that I've spent on that staff I have had the opportunity to work with a Jazz Mass, and go on several mission trips. I've attended several national meetings of the Episcopal Church and have been impressed with the creativity and energy that I found in those events. The Men's Bible Class that is believed to be over 100 years old continues to be an active group of men who meet every other week to share breakfast and study of the upcoming lessons for the following Sunday. I was both a presenter and staff to that group, but was also a fully involved member and when my wife was in the hospital and later died they were there for me as a community in a way that I would never forget. I very much appreciate the support I felt from

Randy and the rest of the staff and it was a great way to come to the end of that phase in my life.

During the years that followed, Sandra was in regular treatment. Most people would have had no indication that she was spending hours a week in the local cancer center for transfusions. She would feel the increasing effects of low energy, but she went on with her life as best she could.

Before she became terribly ill, we tried several different things. Camping had always been an interest in our family though Sandra had not enjoyed the tent camping as much. So I came up with the idea of getting an Air Stream Camper that would allow us to travel around in retirement until we found a place that we might want to settle. We had some years earlier bought a condo in Blowing Rock, North Carolina a place that we both enjoyed for our family vacations as well as our own get away. It was a bit far from our home in Richmond, too far for a weekend place but we traveled down when we could and the kids enjoyed our place as well. With the Air Stream came the need for a big Dodge truck and the adventures of trying to tow and park a trailer, a new experience for both of us. We had a great trip to Niagara Falls; we camped right on the river that led to the Falls. Then another summer one of our daughters, Laura, joined me in driving the truck and trailer to Maine and we flew Sandra up to join us. We had a nice trip, but the reality of her illness became apparent and when I came home from that trip I sold the trailer and truck back to the dealer. That was a dream we would not realize beyond that brief time.

We traveled down to Blowing Rock to look there about a retirement home and after a search for housing we decided that the weather and the lack of diversity of the area would not appeal to us in the long run. It was after that visit that we decided to sell the condo as well. I was beginning to realize that I had done good planning to take care of Sandra in the event of my death but had not considered the possibility of her death before mine. I had insurance on my life that would have taken care of her, but when she died I lost her retirement and social security income. Fortunately I had been able to make decisions like selling the condo that allowed me to survive financially after her death. Sandra lived to see two of our daughters through their weddings and we participated in welcoming our first grand child Claire into the world.

A year before her death, we went to University of Maryland Medical Center for a second opinion on treatment options. The conclusion was much the same, though a new drug was recommended and her local doctor followed through with that treatment. In the course of that treatment, she developed an infection and almost died. While she was in the hospital, she had to miss our daughter Katie's wedding shower, but we "Skyped" her in so she was able to be part of the party. She eventually recovered from that infection and was able to attend the wedding. A year later she was at a point of failing results and she decided to submit to the process of testing for a bone marrow transplant. The doctors who had been so attentive and had treated her with conservative step-by-step care now stepped back, and a more aggressive group of doctors took over the treatment process. A hospitalization was required and treatments administered. She actually did well with the procedure, but developed pneumonia and the attempts to treat it did not work. Finally, she had a series of strokes as a result of the blood work.

But she managed to celebrate her 70th birthday on Wednesday, October 31, 2012 before she died on November 2, 2012. We were there with her to the end. This was the beginning of the first year of grief, but I realized in time that the grief had begun some time before, as we had been preparing for what we could see coming but did not want to acknowledge. In that first year, I would occasionally realize that the cloud that had followed us for those years before was no longer there and I would feel some guilt in the relief. I grieved for her, but not for the feeling that our world had increasingly closed in on us.

The year that followed her death was significant. My usual response to any problem is to read about how other people have faced the issues, and that's exactly what I did. I read books about life after death, near death experiences, books about what the loss of a mother does to her daughters. Three months into the process, I went on a four-day silent retreat in a religious community in Boston. I came home with a deep feeling of peace and joy that I hadn't felt in ages. It was short-lived, but I was hopeful that if I could feel that joy once, surely there would be other times and opportunities.

In the spring, we welcomed the birth of a second granddaughter, Charlotte Sandra Ford, a beautiful, healthy baby girl. The books talk about how much daughters need their mothers at the birth of their children; Charlotte's birth was not an exception. All of us missed Sandra's quiet presence, but Katie had the mixed feelings of delight in her own daughter and sadness at the absence of her mother's care. We were all there for her, but it wasn't the same and could not be. A friend had said to me that she believed that Sandra had held that baby in the weeks before the birth, preparing her for what was to come. It was a comforting thought, and one I wanted to hold onto in that emotional time.

Our daughter, Laura, was married in June. The weddings in our family have been occasions to party and her wedding was no exception. The bride-to-be had gone with her mother to see the location for her wedding, an outdoor gazebo. Mother and daughters had gone wedding dress shopping and Sandra had seen "the dress." She knew what the menu would include and where the flowers would come from. The pastor would be the man who had confirmed all three daughters, had married the other two and had, that past November, been the one to preach at Sandra's memorial service. He had captured her spirit then, and he brought that spirit with him to the wedding. The flowers were exceptional and the girls put together a special bouquet that sat in the empty seat beside me. I was not sure that I wanted that reminder so close in that context, but it was the right choice. A butterfly even hovered around the service and served as a reminder of our hope for the future. The experts say that daughters need their mothers at their weddings, and again they are right. We danced all night and united two families, all the while with an awareness that someone was missing.

We gathered the whole family together for summer vacation in our favorite part of the country, the mountains of North Carolina. We took Sandra's ashes to spread there. My three daughters and I woke early in the morning and left for the lake where we had walked as a family for years. We entered the woods off the path and poured out those gray fragments, holding each other as we prayed together. We know where the ashes are and we can return to connect with her in a place where she had been happy and at peace.

We were halfway through the first year and it was time for something more intense. I sought out a Camino, Spanish for path. Since the 1200s, people have left their regular lives to take time to walk a path for a period of time in reflection and in memorial. In August, Laura, who had married in June, joined me on the Camino de Santiago. The Camino de Santiago has been around since the 13th century AD, and is made up of various trails in France and Spain that lead toward Santiago, Spain. The cathedral there holds the bones of St. James and thousands of people have walked as pilgrims to this shrine. We had hoped to go in October, at the end of the year of our mourning, but Laura could not get away from her teaching position, so we went in August. Because of the heat and the number of tourists in Europe in late summer, we decided to take one of the less traveled routes. We flew into Paris on the first day of August and took a trail down to Toulouse in the Southern part of France, where we started walking from a small town called Auch.

For 15 days, we walked daily for ten to as many as 18 miles, and in the end we had walked at least 170 miles. We carried all of our gear on our backs, each of us carrying a small one-person tent and sleeping gear. Over the years, the trail has developed a series of hostels called GTE's that offer a bed, dinner and a breakfast to those on the walk. When we could find one of these places we stayed; when we could sleep in our tents, we did. As it worked out, we camped about a third of the time, slept in the GTE's another third and in hotels the remainder of the time. The food was fresh and filling, the wine and beer excellent, the coffee and bread were wonderful.

There is nothing quite like the European custom of good breads, jams and strong coffee in the morning. Even now when I go out in the early morning for a run or bike ride I make it a point to stop on the way home for a double espresso in a demitasse cup; the good taste, the cup, the rising sun take me right back to good mornings in Paris or where ever I found myself on those mornings. Each day we would walk and talk, but more often we spent the hours alone with our thoughts.

I had taken five books on my Kindle and read in the afternoon and evenings after we had finished the day's hike. I used the time to think about what I was reading. I reviewed the past and prayed daily for my family and for our future. Just as on the long bike rides of the past, I found that I could drop down below superficial thinking to a deeper place. I carried a journal and when we stopped I wrote about what I was seeing or what my internal process had uncovered. I began to realize that retirement had allowed me to be more available while Sandra was alive and going through treatment, but now I needed something meaningful to fill the extra hours. I had signed up for a writing course before we left and downloaded the text as one of my books. I reflected on what it would be like to devote my extra time to writing. What would I want to convey? Where would the writing take me? The idea of "creative non-fiction writing" seemed perfect for me. I came home hopeful and the course did not disappoint. The day I left for the trip I submitted an article, a year in the writing, on the future of the church. It was not particularly optimistic in tone, and I realized that I wanted to experiment with new ways of expressing and living out faith and in building community. Participating in the start up of the Jazz Mass at our church was a great opportunity to meet that need.

Laura and I also worked at deepening our relationship during the Camino by understanding our different ways of grieving and what it meant to have mutual respect. At the beginning of the walk, I felt that she was angry with me and I finally said something to her. She was angry. She did not think that I missed my wife--her mother--as much as I should. She felt that I had not thought through the details of this trip. I talked about the ways I compartmentalized my feelings. When I put the feelings into a box and onto the shelf, they remain there until something shakes the box open. For her, the feelings were always in play. We talked about different ways of expressing our feelings. I admitted that I depended on her to figure out how this trip was going to unfold. She had traveled in Europe more than I. Her language skills in French and Spanish were essential and I was in the position of following her lead, a role reversal that was testing but valuable in the end to both of us. We hiked through the Pyrenees into Spain and came to the end of our trip after a train ride across Spain to Santiago and Finisterre (the end of the earth).

Santiago is an amazing town. Narrow streets that wind around to the Cathedral are filled with vendors. Each day a group of pilgrims arrives in the main square, their trip complete. Laura and I went into the church and decided to attend an English Mass. The Priest was Irish and on vacation. He invited various ones in the congregation to participate; I read the psalm for the day. His homily was funny and appropriate for the finish of the trip. At the end of the Mass he invited those interested to come to a café behind the church for coffee and conversation. There was a sense of common adventure and a conclusion of a special trip.

We came home to pick up our lives where we left off. It will take more time to sort out the import of our trip, but I ended with a sense of hope for the future and that same taste of joy that I had experienced after leaving the silent retreat. I looked forward to the writing course and to the work that lay ahead.

I have tried over this year to keep myself open to my feelings, to share them with others, to push myself into uncomfortable places, and to use reading as a way of opening to deeper feelings. I have continued to journal and to keep up my yoga practice, to look for time to be with family when the opportunity presents, and I have felt their caring presence. During the year, I have come up in the regular preaching schedule several times and have incorporated into those sermons some of my experience with grief and faith.

In the fall, another grandchild was born, Jay Cooper Porter, the first boy. He is called "Cooper." Our family came together again to celebrate his birth. Some time after that Laura and Jimmy told us that they were expecting their first child in June of 2014. Life continues to move forward.

So on November the 2nd we came to the end of the first year without Sandra. We'd made it that far; we were still intact as a family. We had cleaned Sandra's clothes out of the house and I had settled any matters of the estate that had been unresolved. I had finalized my own plans for my funeral. We approached Christmas reminded again of Sandra's love for the season: the decorations, her tree, and the enjoyment she received from buying clothes for her children. Grief turns out to be more like a series of waves than a straight line. I can go for some time without feeling the loss and then suddenly from nowhere will come a reminder and the feelings will be there just under the surface ready to emerge out of the box and back onto the floor. We did not have a perfect marriage; I know that I let my wife down in many ways, and she was not always what I needed her to be. But we decided to hang in there through all that came and we stayed married to the end.

We have three grown children who have moved into their own lives. I watch them raising their own children and marvel at their wisdom and patience. I have work that I enjoy and continue to find ways of learning and growing. I do not feel that I have finished; in fact I think that I am preparing for the next adventure, ready to step out into the unknown.

Early in 2015 I made the decision to sell the house I lived in. I had enjoyed the Fan, the community where we had found a 100-year-old town house. I had been able to make it more ecologically acceptable and Sandra had supervised the installation of a garden in the back of the house. But, it was 3,000 square feet and more room than I needed. I invited the kids to pick out the furniture they wanted to keep. I went through a process of looking at everything that I owned and deciding weather or not I "loved" it enough to keep it. In my typical way I have found a book, *The Life-Changing Magic of Tidying Up* by Marie Kondo, that was just the right process at the right time. The house sold quickly that spring and now I asked myself what to do. My original plan had been to store what was left and to live simply with the goal of landing in New York City in the fall to take more courses. But, the concept evolved into something quite different. I ended up buying a one-bedroom condo in another old community in Richmond. It has great storage for the camping and biking gear, a covered garage for the car and a nice open living space with an exposed ceiling and lots of light from the windows at the end of the unit. It has turned out to be an interesting part of the adventure. I am discovering a new part of the city, I can walk to the grocery, to places to eat and have coffee, even to the doctor's office. I can lock the door and leave without concern.

And leave I did. I finished my work as an Interim Associate Rector at St. James' after a year of full time work. Leaving so many people that I care deeply for and who were community for me was not easy. I needed to distance myself for a period of time to let the new associate make her way unimpeded and I will return to the pew there some time in the New Year. I left the afternoon after the last sermon and service for a month long trip to Europe, the Czech Republic, London and a time in London. I came home to leave again on another long bike ride on the Blue Ridge Parkway and have been to Boston and to Cape Cod learning how to enjoy not being on a schedule or needing to show up at a desk for the first time in many years.

I decided that had taken enough courses. I enjoyed the on-line connection and the weekly writing requirements, but I needed to work on this book. So I found a coach and got to work and we'll see where this comes out. Like other experiences in my life this is turning out to be adult education. I am learning as I go. I have continued to read widely and have become more able to read critically not only from the content but also from a perspective of style. Becoming comfortable identifying myself as a "writer" and letting that stand by itself has been a growing awareness and hopefully a sense of direction for the years ahead.

What Can You Do to Tend Toward Generativity Rather Than Stagnation?

This is a long stage of adulthood and you may find that you go in and out of being in times of generativity and then stagnation. It is important to recognize what is happening as it is happening, you can slide into an easy time in life that isn't challenging you to become more of who you are created to be. There are also risks involved, especially when you have achieved success in a particular field or profession. To stir the pot and take a risk is very real. You might find that you could experiment with new behaviors or activities with lower risk. Teach a class at church, take an art or photography class, go camping or take an unusual vacation, shake up your routine—it may lead to greater change or it may bring excitement back to the routine you have fallen into.

QUESTIONS FOR STAGE SEVEN

1. What are the high points in your life to date?
2. Did you feel that you made decisions for your life, or did circumstances, or your work force you to make decisions that were not in your best interest?
3. Do you have a Bucket List of things that you need to accomplish before you would be ready to finish?
4. Have your values and opinions changed over time? Are you more open and trusting or are you anxious about the future?
5. Have you had to deal with losses? What have your learned from the experience?

STAGE EIGHT: EGO INTEGRITY VS. DESPAIR

> "Only in him who in some way has taken care of things and people and has adapted himself to the triumphs and disappointments adherent in being, the originator of others or the generator of products and ideas-only in him may gradually ripe the fruit of these seven stages."
> Erik H. Erikson, *Childhood and Society*

Somewhere along the way Erikson's stage of Generativity Vs. Stagnation merges into the last stage; Integrity Vs. Despair. Moving to a true sense of retirement signals that move to consideration of what remains to be done in life. Generativity is still a part of life at this stage. But for those who have not risked doing what they needed to do in life, it is time to face the music. Despair is not depression; it is to "be without hope," in other words, to come to the last stage of life and feel that you had not lived, not done what you needed to do and come to a realization that time is running out. Throughout one's life you come to crossroads, decision that have to be made all of those decisions add up to the integrity of one's life. At this stage in life it's time to add it up. Are you satisfied with your life? Is there more ahead for you? Are you willing to risk what it will take to feel satisfied with your life? We don't know the hour or the day, but it is closer now than ever before.

The epic journeys of my life have been highlights, moments in time when for a minute I stepped out of character for a few days, cut loose from the comforts of regular suburban life, carried all that I had on my bike or on my back. I have learned how to enter a place of deep thought, and also that I can take a risk and survive. I will fall down, will fail, will stand back up and press on; I may arrive at a different place than the one I aimed for, and I can explain that only through the eyes of faith.

When your heart takes its first beat, when you draw that first breath, you begin to move forward. I do not believe that the movement is pointless. I do believe that we have free will and can make turns and stops that take us off course, but that somehow there is a purpose there waiting to be discovered; family, community, those closest the ones we marry or take fully into our lives become part of that quest, that forward movement. People who come to the end of life and feel that it has run out before they had the courage to act come to despair. They are as afraid of dying as they have been of living. Integrity is not an isolated act at the end of life, but rather a combination of decisions made, risks taken, a process of self-discovery that comes to an end with the sense that life has been lived not without need for some measure of forgiveness, but lived fully within the bounds you found yourself. To the people who would say of the bike rides or the hike, "I wish I could do that," my response was always, "Come on."

I want to keep saying that to myself, to keep pushing to understand what is ahead, to reach toward the next challenge, the next risk, the next "come on." I want to come to that last breath not unlike the first: unsure of what is ahead but moving toward the light.

So I am coming to the end of this story, and hopefully it is not the end but a new beginning. For a long time I've been "at work" for someone, some institution, even for my self. I have needed to show up and to stay until the job was done or the day was at end. I've had some great experiences, met some great people, and together we have done great things.

So is it going to be three strikes and you are out? Or can we change the rules? Hopefully you have been playing by some rules all along and we can now focus on expanding those rules, getting the most out of life. For some age 70 is the new 50. Many people are living well into the 80's or 90's. How to do that well is now our focus. Quantity of life is not as important as the Quality of that life. What do you need to finish? What do you need to start? What are you passing on to the next generations other than your assets? How will you be remembered? Is it the way you want to be remembered? The new science has determined that our brains can grow and change into old age, but it takes courage and effort.

SO CAN WE CHANGE THE RULES?

The title of this memoir is *Mapping Your Adventure: Discovering Integrity in a Life Review*. My writing to this point has been a walk through how I got to 70 and beyond. The question now is one of changing the rules for the future. Clearly more of us are living longer than expected. The question is one of what difference that makes or is there a way to live it in a more meaningful way? As my story indicates there have been amazing changes in the last 100 years. We survived two world wars; we witnessed the invention of air travel, the Internet, a global awareness of what is happening here and around the world. The concepts of work and family, quality of life, ethics, belief have all been under great pressure to change and adapt to the movement of science and technology. From the birth control pill to the personal computer to the global economy, the models we were born with for work and family life have been blown apart and we are trying to find our way. Over the years I have attempted to read widely and to think about what is happening to us, what we can do about our experience. I don't have all the answers, but in the pages ahead I will attempt to share some skills and techniques from what I've learned over the last 70+ years and I look forward to conversations with you about what you've learned, how we can grow into this new era together.

One of many books by Daniel Siegel, M.D. is entitled *The Pocket Guide to Interpersonal Neurobiology: an Integrative Handbook*. In this book he outlines aspects of our life that support neuroplasticity. His research and that of others demonstrates that our brains can continue to grow and change well into our later years. Another leader in the field is Jon Kabat-Zinn, a professor of medicine emeritus at the University of Massachusetts. He has over 30 years developed an eight-week course that taught people who suffered with chronic pain ways to manage pain through meditation, yoga and exercise. His book *Full Catastrophe Living* outlined his method. Over the years the work he demonstrated has been confirmed by new developments in the science of brain study. With Functional Magnetic Resonance Imagery testing we can watch the brain react to input and can see clear physical growth in the brain. I will draw on the various aspects that he holds up as being important.

HEALTH

It is clear to me that when I am healthy everything else can be managed. When I 'm not feeling well it colors everything. Chronic illness affects every aspect of a person's life. So first and foremost is the issue of maintaining our health. If you are NOT into some form of exercise stop reading this book, put on your shoes and go for a walk! It is clear from everything I read and from my own experience that regular exercise of some form is extremely important. I first discovered it as a therapist when I found myself with a depressed client. There are medications for depression and I don't depreciate their benefits. A doctor needs to prescribe and monitor these. But for most of us just getting outside and moving can raise our emotional health. I had always enjoyed being out doors, on my bike, hiking or playing games.

But first I needed to face up to my smoking. On December 6, 1981 I quit smoking. I started in college and had smoked a pack a day for years. Sandra had told me to quit "stopping" on our vacations: I was making everyone miserable and I would go back to smoking when I went back to work. I was told that if you should quit on your birthday, the astrological signs would favor that change. The other suggestion was that when you are starting a new job is a good time to change behaviors. I was getting ready to move to Washington Hospital Center to a new job and that did the trick. I haven't had a cigarette since.

At 25 I first began serious exercise. I had started with the Canadian Royal Air Force Exercise Program when I was an Intern in Memphis. This program had a daily set of drills that you did everyday until you reached your age and fitness level. I began work at it and after a time reached that level and maintained for some years. Once you reached your level you could stay there and only go through the exercises three times a week. That was the beginning for me. I had started running about the same time. Sandra was getting ready to go back to her high school 20th anniversary and she decided that she would start running to get ready. She did and she looked great, but she hated running and stopped as soon as we got home from that party. I on the other hand started running and grew to love it. Walking was my wife's activity. We enjoyed our daily walks together when we could and later long hikes as well. It is so easy: just a comfortable pair of good shoes and you can get as crazy as you need to about the clothes, as you want to. But good shoes are important: don't go cheap—get ones that fit and don't wear them forever. I change my running shoes every six months. I have two pairs and alternate them on runs, and I pay good money for my shoes from a reputable running store.

I have for many years been a long distance bike rider. But I started running because it takes less time to have a good workout. When I run, I only need some shorts and a good pair of shoes. For years, I have moved back and forth between running and biking; however, I did not become a real runner until a couple of years ago, when I decided to join a group of people training for a local half-marathon. When I run with a group, the time passes so quickly I hardly notice the miles, the heat, the rain, or whatever else comes my way. I finished right at the end of two hours. I felt great but changed.

I had always seen myself as plodder, a runner who was not sleek or long-legged, more of a finisher than a racer. On this day my self-image changed. Even after a bike accident that crushed my leg (three pins and a piece of cadaver bone, a year of recovery), when I ran a recent half-marathon I finished in 2 hours and 18 minutes, sixth in my age group.

At age 70 I had become a runner! It is also true that at my age you can place if you just show up. To me there is nothing quite like a good long run or bike ride. Once my body has warmed up I can begin to enjoy the world around me, I can start to think through a topic or problem and work it from the beginning to the end.

I'm still biking and just finished a 300-mile trip on the Blue Ridge Parkway, maybe some of the hardest riding I've ever done. There is nothing like getting on my bike and out the door. I will often find myself thinking about how much I'm enjoying myself and if I look at the odometer I'll usually find out that I'm right at the 5 mile point. I'm warmed up and ready to go as long as I have time to ride. Add camping to that and we have an epic journey you can count me in on.

Everyone says that you should go get a doctor's permission if you haven't been exercising before you start. At the risk of some law suit I would say don't use that as an excuse to avoid starting. Start listening to your body; when you get tired stop and rest. Don't expect to walk for miles when you start out. Add 10% to your distance every week. See how far you get in a ½ hour. See if you can increase the distance, look at your surroundings, and greet the other people you'll meet out there. For me it has helped to have a destination or a route that I wanted to walk.

Another recommendation is to consider a Fitbit or some other walking measurement program. I like the Fitbit because it downloads to the computer and I get a weekly daily report of my distance (I only look at it weekly), but I find that just knowing that I have my Fitbit on causes me to walk more, climb more stairs. I have added on people with whom I compete. Every week several friends and a couple of my children's weekly totals show up and I know where I stand. I've moved from the simple clip on model to the one that also measures my sleep pattern and I even have the Fitbit scale that measures my weight and body composition, but by now you already know that I'm a little crazy about this exercise stuff.

Swimming and bike riding are alternatives to walking or running. If your bones aren't up to the pounding, the pool or the bike are great alternatives. One of my brothers swims daily. For me any day that starts with a bike ride is a good day! In my six years as Director of Pastor Care at the Medical College Of Virginia I didn't have a parking pass for most of the time. When the weather was too bad for the bike I could walk three blocks to catch a bus. The longer rides on the weekend are a treat. I have a regular group of riders that I join for the longer rides. They are important community for me (more about that later), but they also challenge me to ride longer and faster than I might on my own. There is clothing available that both pads your bottom and keeps you going in hot and cold weather. In Virginia I've been able to ride almost year round. Ice on the road isn't a great incentive but rain, cold, wind, heat are opportunities to overcome.

The main thing to think about when you are getting a bike is finding one that fits! Most studies show that if the bike isn't comfortable you won't ride it. It helps to go to a store where the people know how to find a bike that fits you. There are all sorts of bikes now available, from entry level to the most expensive. After a certain point what you are paying for is weight reduction. You need to decide what your intent is and who you might be riding with.

I have three bikes. One is a mountain bike with shocks

and big tires; it's like riding in a Caddie, slow, heavy and safe on the leaves and gravel. I don't go on the off road without a partner anymore, but it is just very comfortable. My second bike is a great commuter bike. It has fenders and a full range of gears. It is very comfortable. I can pull a one-wheel trailer behind this bike with my tent and all the gear for a long trip. It's not fast, but it is steady. Then I have a racing bike. I've never been a racer, but this bike is light and responsive and when I join the group for a long ride I can hang in there with them. We ride and talk and life is good.

I could go on forever about exercise. Hopefully you get the point. Don't wait, put your excuses aside and get out there.

DIET

Eating well is the most confusing of topics for me. Over the years and especially on the long bike trips and the Camino that my daughter and I hiked, I found that eating little or no meat or chicken has proven to be helpful. I have always had a weight problem. My grandmother pointed it out in a shaming way, but I've been aware of it and on some sort of diet since junior high. Even with the exercise I fight to keep within bounds and always feel that I need to lose 10 pounds. Food is an important as a connector to people. Good restaurants, conversation, beer, and wine add to the pleasure. I also like desserts and chocolate. I don't know what to say about this topic, except that is clear that keeping your weight down to an appropriate level is important. If you have family history of heart, diabetic or cancer problems it is clear that diet figures in to prevention and if need be treatment. The fact that my grandfathers died at age 63 of heart attacks and then my dad had open-heart surgery at the same age was a wake up call for me. No matter how much exercise, diet, sleep you get, you have to figure in it's hard to beat genetics. Researching your family history can be very helpful and might motivate you to consider changes in life style.

While we are on that subject I have a particular rant. We are constantly bombarded on our TVs about all the drugs that are available to fix whatever ails us. What that has meant is a society of people who believes that their health is someone else's responsibility. We don't have to worry when we become sick; we just have to get to the doctor who will know what to do to fix us right up. There's a pill or a surgery for everything. My father-in-law late in his life was taking over 20 medications a day. When I asked him what they were for he had no idea. At the end of his life he knew the end was near and he quit taking the daily ritual of pills and for the last weeks of life felt better than he had for months. I've worked for over 17 years of my professional life in and around hospitals. I know they can do great things. My wife's extended life and the quality of that life was a result of good medicine and care. But avoiding medication is better than adding on pills for whatever comes.

Back to that idea about putting down this book and getting out for a walk do what you can to hold on to your health!

THERAPY

I mention at various points in my story the feelings I had of depression. When you come out of a period of depression you realize what life had been like. My first experience in a therapeutic experience with Bob Lantz was revealing and transformational for me. Later in the parish and in my residency I continued to be in a therapeutic relationship. But it was later in my life that entered a longer-term therapy. When I moved into the second half of my work at Washington Hospital Center I had the financial resources to seek out a therapist. I intentionally sought out a woman and I benefited greatly from that six-year relationship. I was married to a woman, had three daughters, and a not so great relationship with my mother, so I had a lot to sort out. It was a very gradual process of weekly conversation that helped me grow in understanding my conscious and unconscious actions and myself. I reached a point of conclusion and I greatly benefited from that long-term relationship.

SLEEP
For years I have prided myself on the idea that I only needed six hours of sleep on a daily basis. Recent research has proven the need for seven or eight hours is not only for good health but for good decision making and relationships. I had to make a conscious effort to change my sleeping habits, to get to bed earlier, to get my sleeping space darker, cooler. But it has paid off. I can tell a difference in the way I feel when I've had enough sleep. I know that I am a safer driver as a result. I am also learning how to enjoy a couple of 10-minute naps on a daily basis. When my brain feels tired, I take a brief nap. It is an amazing pick-me-up and good sleep affects the rest of my life.

COMMUNITY
It is clear from looking back over my life that I have existed in continuous community. From the family I was born into and into the church that was lead by my dad I was never far from people who cared for me. Leaving home

for college was a step toward becoming an adult, but even that step was with the assistance to the college family, the fraternity, friends, and faculty. Even in that time I was active to a degree in the local church. I didn't have extra income so often the dates that Sandra and I enjoyed were to church activities, including our first dates to Lenten Wednesday night services. At least she had some idea what she was getting into. Later the parish after my first year of seminary was a grace filled place for me. My first parish, Christ the King in S. Miami and its counter part Christ the King in Richmond were places where we found connection and affection. The move to Northern Virginia included membership at Lord of Life Lutheran Church and over 20 years of pastoral care, teaching and leadership in preaching and worship. Our family was surrounded and supported by caring people and we gave back our affection and care for our friends in those parishes. The move to Richmond was enhanced by our connection to St. James' Episcopal church and later my service on staff there. The Men's Bible Class that has been meeting for 100 years was a place where I found a home and in the midst of my wife's death they surrounded me and held me up. I could not imagine life without connection to those communities.

But there is community to be had in many places. I am part of a group called the Torch Club that meets monthly to hear a paper read and to share a paper by one of our members. A couple of times a week now I play Petanque, a French ball game like the Italian Bocce game. The United States runs on the backs of clubs and churches that provide service and support to the community. Like the group of men I ride bikes with on a weekly basis, it is a place to be known to reach out and find others concerned and caring.

As a now single person I have noticed that women seem to have a greater capacity for friendship with other women. It is not unusual for two women to go out for dinner or to a movie and to enjoy the conversation and intimacy of the friendship. I find it not as easy for me as a single male. For now it seems not a thing that men do with each other and when it's with a woman it may be innocent, but it seems like a date. I do feel that it's not much fun to go out to dinner alone. I will take a book and read while I'm there, but to be surrounded by couples enjoying themselves adds to the aloneness. Having regular connections to others is very important and adds to the quality of life.

It seems that in some ways our access to the Internet and to phone and e-mail connection is a way of staying in touch and connected. But more people are working in long distance connections and don't have the natural connection to community at work. People who are self-employed and otherwise working on their computers may need to be more intentional about seeking out community. Churches are in many cases losing members and congregations are not attracting younger people. The idea of an automatic connection to a church that was expected in an earlier day is gone and finding lasting connection to a worshiping community is sometimes difficult. But it is worth the effort.

As a newly single person a question of finding another relationship is new territory. All three of my daughter's were successful in finding meaningful relationship online. So I decided to follow their lead and met interesting people and one in particular. Starting late in life on a new relationship means there's a lot of baggage to unpack and complicated connections for it all to work out. Having been in a successful relationship in the past encouraged me to seek out a new relationship, someone to share life with and this time when I talk about a life of adventure I have a better idea what that might include.

NOVELTY

Changing the rules means looking at everything with new eyes. Over the years my wife and I moved from apartment to apartment and then to house after house. We ended in a very nice town home in an historic community. It had three bed rooms, a living room, dining room, study, kitchen and den about 3,000 square feet in all. The yard was small and manageable and we had fixed the place up nicely. But in looking at it some time after my wife's death I realized that I did not need all that space and taking care of the furniture and the house was not where I needed to be. I had also been through sorting out the estates of my in-laws and my aunt in the past and did not want to leave a burden like that to my children. So I moved in a new direction. In preparing to sell the house the real estate agent brought in a woman who made suggestions to stage the house. Essentially that meant taking a lot of stuff out of the house. As I mentioned, I used a book by Marie Kondo entitled *The Life-Changing Magic Of Tidying Up: the Japanese Art of Decluttering and Organizing*. She encourages a practice of removing groups of things like your books all into one room, then picking up each book and asking the question, do I love this book or not. If the answer is yes, keep it. If no, the book goes out the door. I removed 21 boxes of books from my library and still had plenty of books left. My town house took on a new look of openness and when I moved to my new condo I held on to that minimal look. For now I've decided to clean the house myself and every other week or so I try to look intentionally at all the stuff I still have to dust and take care of. So far it has been a meaningful process.

Taking up a new hobby, reading in a different field, joining a different group, travel—whatever it is that brings new experience to life is a routine breaker that keeps our minds growing and alert. The Internet offers easy ways to explore opportunities. Just plug in an interest and information comes to your fingertips, then it's a matter of discernment, what do you want to do next and what is keeping you from a new adventure.

JOURNALING

As I mentioned earlier in the book when I took my first long bike ride across the United State I began a daily practice of journaling. I begin everyday with my journal and a cup of hot lemon water (someone told me that it was good for you and it hasn't hurt me). A lot of time the journal is banal. I did this or that yesterday whatever, but some days it is amazing what comes from nowhere. I have journals filled with illegible script that I weed out periodically. It's not written for anyone else and it has been a window into my thinking over these many years. I have found that the writing process helps me understand myself at a deeper level.

YOGA/MEDITATION

The journaling led to the whole process of having a regular yoga practice. I started that early as well and now either meditate for a period of time or practice my own yoga course. All this means that I have to get up early, ahead of anything that I have planned like a run or bike ride.

It's made me more intentional about getting to bed early to get the sleep necessary. No one said that this was easy or without some effort. But, the benefits are significant. I am not as reactive or impulsive as I might otherwise be. I have a chance to think through things.

The quiet end of the yoga session is a gift. I was introduced to Yoga as a form of stretching and meditation. The running and long distance bike rides came along with it. I then moved into a more complex stretching model and from that to Yoga. The gym that I had joined in DC that allowed me to get into the city early and to workout before work had a program to certify one as a personal trainer. I took that course. That course became the foundation for a 300-hour yoga instructor course. I worked through it and was certified as a yoga instructor and for some years taught at the Down Town YMCA. I was also the official yoga instructor for Bike Virginia for several years.

I have become more aware over time of my thinking and feeling processes. For some Centering Prayer is the answer. Meditation instruction is available in many churches and communities. For others like my parents simply beginning everyday reading a devotional tract over their breakfast and before the newspaper was a centering process.

HUMOR

Finally, it helps to have a sense of humor. Writer Norman Cousins cured himself from cancer by leaving the hospital, going to a motel and watching stacks of funny movies. Science is discovering that people benefit from laughter and from letting go of some of the strain of life. When my family of origin all get together there always seems to be a lot of joking back and forth. We share common political and religious beliefs and the humor is often connected to those beliefs and our hopes for the future. We don't get together very often and after a time together I regret that we aren't more intentional about those times. But where ever it comes finding the humor in life is important. I start everyday reading the funny papers. Dagwood and Dennis along with Rex Morgan and others leave me with something to laugh about some time open new insight into life for me. My connection to my grandchildren is a new experience and the joy that I feel after a time with them is very meaningful.

There is much being discovered about the connection between our emotions and our overall health and wellbeing. When I first began my work as a hospital chaplain we were already noticing connections between our emotions and our health. We would record the visits and collect stories but had no way to prove that those connections made a difference. That objective proof is now becoming available and we are looking at quality of life, the effects of stress as well as the connections to our sub-conscious and un-conscious thinking.

FAITH
What have you come to believe in and what's important to you?

Finally there is the issue of what I believe, where my faith comes out. I discovered in my work as a therapist that theology was not often a part of the conversation until the end of a therapeutic journey. Then it seemed that the language and reflection of religious tradition was useful in describing what my client and I had experienced. Moving deeply into someone's life, having someone move into my own life gave me the sense that there is a spiritual force at work, something beyond what I would be capable of by myself.

Over the years of working in various congregations from my first in Columbia, South Carolina, to Christ the King in Miami, Christ the King in Richmond, Lord of Life in Fairfax and now St. James', I have found myself connected to a community that supported and sustained me. In the last four years or so preaching in a regular rotation, deeply involved in a creative Jazz worship format, celebrating the Eucharist, hearing confession and extending absolution has had a profound effect on me. Jesus talks at times about a feeling of compassion for the people who followed him from place to place. His touch and words are healing for people. I have had the privilege of connecting to that experience. I have felt the healing benefit of being surrounded by family and friends in the midst of the loss of my wife. I have experienced the joy of celebrating new life as I splashed water on the heads of my newly born grandchildren, and on my own children as well. When I looked over the altar rail into the faces of the people sitting in the congregation I knew from my experience of them that there were people there suffering through all sorts of concerns in their lives. The feeling of compassion that I felt for those people is something beyond anything I could feel on my own. I feel that I have had the privilege of being with people at meaningful points in their lives. I have been able to reflect on the scripture in sermons in away that shared the new insight I was gaining from that study. The chances I've had to lead adult study have also been a time of dialogue. I have risked sharing what I was discovering and have been challenged to present my ideas in ways that connect with others and to learn from their insights, from the courage they manifest in the way they live their lives. There is no simple answer, no formula other than the most basic: love God, love your neighbor as you love yourself. Working that out on a daily basis is the work of faith in action.

The church may be losing ground right now, but the community of the church has always been important. I think that clergy need more training in effective ways of providing pastoral care and in looking at the ways groups within the church may function more intentionally. As our world becomes increasingly global and at the same time disconnected, finding places of meaningful connection will be coming increasingly important and attractive. A recent book entitled *The Healthy Churches' Handbook: A Process for Revitalizing Your Church* by Robert Warren describes the growth of the Church of England congregations in and around London. The growth has been significant and the theory suggests that when people are invited to create the type of community they want they will return to the abandoned buildings of the past.

All of your life you have been making decisions and now it's time to look over your life with a critical eye. Have you done what you needed to do? Engaging in a "life review" can happen at any time in a person's life. A teenager could sit for a while and reflect on their childhood and what they have accomplished, maybe as they prepare applications for a job or for entrance into college of graduate school. In mid-life losing a job or going through a divorce or other life crisis can be a hard time but also a time to reflect on who you are and what you have done with your life. Beginning to look at what you need to finish is important. We all know people whose life ended unexpectedly, in an accident, or in a life ending disease. We grieve for those lost relationships but we are also grieving for the unfinished trajectory of their lives, what they would have accomplished had their lives continued to a natural end. Even if you have come to what looks like the end of your life, it is not to late to think about what you need to say to those around you, to finish unfinished business, to say the things you need to say. Despair is to be without hope. There is always hope—not necessarily hope for what you would have liked but for doing what you need to do to tie up lose ends and to end well.

It is an exciting time to be alive. For me it is a great time to explore not only more of the world around me, but to read and to think deeply. I have the opportunity to join closely with my children and now grandchildren. Watching these little ones grow and change is significant, as is watching how my daughters are working out their relationships sharing lives with the men in their lives. I am proud of them and hopeful about the future.

At any time of life you might usefully to do a life review. I'm not at the end and will see what lies ahead. But this review is a start. I haven't lived a perfect life. I've made a lot of mistakes. But in the end I'm satisfied. I have few regrets. I look forward to what is ahead with hope and confidence. I invite you to think about your own life. What are the shaping influences in your past? When did you come to cross roads that made significant differences in how your life unfolded? How do you feel life has treated you? Do you feel that your life is leading to a general sense of Integrity or are you running out of time with a lot of unfinished business? What are you doing to maintain your health, what are you avoiding or excusing? Hopefully you can discover the Integrity in your own life.

All the best to you!

ABOUT THE AUTHOR

Dr. Cooper was born in North Carolina and spent the first ten years of his life there. His family moved to Austin, Texas where he finished High School. He grew up in the Lutheran Church and attended Lenoir Rhyne College in Hickory, NC. He attended Lutheran Theological Southern Seminary in Columbia, S.C. where he received a Master's of Divinity degree in 1970. Dr. Cooper completed an Internship and a Residency in Clinical Pastoral Education and is a certified Supervisor in the Association of Clinical Pastoral Education. He was a Diplomat in the American Association of Pastoral Counselors. Dr. Cooper completed a Doctorate of Ministry Degree at Union Seminary in Richmond, VA. He was ordained as a Lutheran Clergy in 1970. His first book is entitled *Get A Life: A Second Chance After Fifty*.

Dr. Cooper was married to Sandra Lynn Greene for 45 years and he has three daughters and five grandchildren. He currently lives in Richmond, VA where he regularly rides his bike, runs, practices yoga and writes.

www.ingramcontent.com/pod-product-compliance
Lightning Source LLC
LaVergne TN
LVHW041542070426
835507LV00011B/887